Pope John Paul II and Pope Benedict XVI

Pope John Paul II and Pope Benedict XVI

KEEPERS OF THE FAITH

SUSAN PROVOST BELLER

FRANKLIN WATTS
A Division of Scholastic Inc.
New York Toronto London Auckland Sydney
Mexico City New Delhi Hong Kong
Danbury, Connecticut

All Photographs © 2007: AP/Wide World Photos: 65, 90 (Pier Paolo Cito), 89 (Jasper Juinen), 72 (KNA), 30 (Claudio Luffoli), 48 (Andrew Medichini), cover bottom right (Martin Meissner), 6 (Christopher Morris), 87 (Massimo Sambucetti/Pool), 84 (Domenico Stinellis), 18, 23, 44; Corbis Images: 67 (Kai Pfaffenbach/Reuters), 2, 38, 83 (Bettmann), 98 (Pier Paolo Cito), cover center (Gianni Giansanti), 29 (Gianni Giansanti/Sygma), 26 (David Lees), 68 (Arturo Mari/Osservatore Romano/Reuters), cover background (Sergio Pitamitz/zefa), 25 (Vittoriano Rastelli), 81 (Reuters TV/Reuters), 58 (Osservatore Romano), 52 (Osservatore Romano/Reuters), 78 (Karen Tweedy-Holmes); Getty Images: 62 (AFP), 9, 11 (Laski Diffusion), 96 (Cindy Karp/Time Life Pictures), 13 (Keystone/Hulton Archive), 61 (STF/AFP), 94 (Time Magazine/Time & Life Pictures); The Image Works: 36 (Wesley Bocxe), 93 (Sean Cayton).

Library of Congress Cataloging-in-Publication Data
Beller, Susan Provost, 1949–
  Pope John Paul II and Pope Benedict XVI : keepers of the faith / by Susan Provost Beller.
      p. cm. — (Great life stories)
  Includes bibliographical references and index.
  ISBN-10: 0-531-13908-5 (lib. bdg.)   0-531-17847-1 (pbk.)
  ISBN-13: 978-0-531-13908-0 (lib. bdg.)   978-0-531-17847-8 (pbk.)
  1. John Paul II, Pope, 1920–2005. 2. Benedict XVI, Pope, 1927– 3. Popes—Biography. I. Title. II. Series.
  BX1378.5.B45 2006
  282.092'2—dc22   2005030645

    2 3 4 5 6 7 8 9 10 R 16 15 14 13 12 11 10 09 08 07

Contents

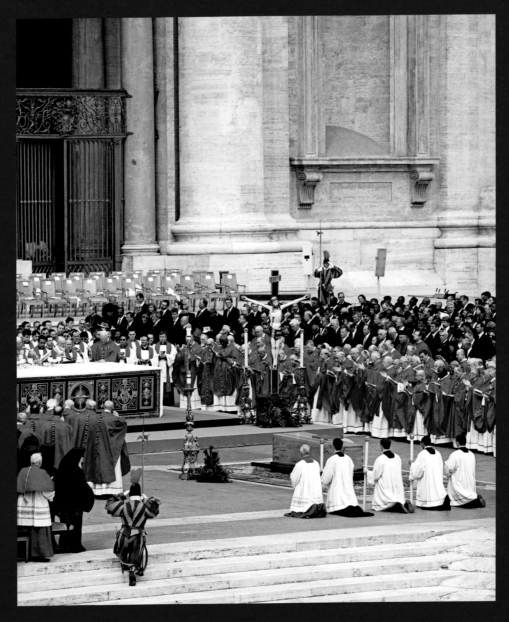

The funeral of Pope John Paul II on Friday, April 8, 2005, was attended by more than a half a million people including dignitaries and church officials. Millions of people converged on Rome to pay their last respects to the pope.

ONE

Karol Wojtyla—the Child, the Actor, the Scholar

Kings, queens, more than fifty heads of state, church officials in their bright red robes, guards in colorful uniforms, more than five hundred thousand spectators, millions of television viewers from around the world—all were focused on a simple cypress wood casket in St. Peter's Square in Rome, Italy. The casket, with a book of Gospels resting on it, was decorated with a simple cross and the letter *M* for Mary, the Mother of God. In this casket lay the body of Karol Wojtyla, known to the world as Pope John Paul II, the head of the Roman Catholic Church. Alongside the body lay the rogito, a document telling of his life and achievements. In the crypt under St. Peter's Basilica, where the casket would later be buried, a handful of dirt from his hometown in Poland was added. The document and the symbolic dirt were testimony to one man's truly remarkable life.

THE MAN

Karol Wojtyla was born on May 18, 1920, in Wadowice, a town near Krakow in southern Poland. Like most residents of the town, the Wojtylas were Catholic and lived side by side with a thriving Jewish community. Karol's father, Karol Sr., a noncommissioned officer in the Polish army, worked as a clerk. He retired from the army as a captain when Karol was seven years old. Well regarded by everyone in town, Karol Sr. was known for his integrity and intelligence.

Karol's mother, Emilia, had attended a convent school and hoped her son would become a priest. She nicknamed Karol "Lolek" and his brother, Edmund, "Mundek." Edmund was thirteen when Karol was born, and he was away at medical school when Karol was young. A sister, Olga, had been born six years before Karol but had died as an infant. The family lived in a cramped but comfortable second-floor apartment close to the church where little Karol would go to pray every day before school.

Lolek excelled at the local grammar school and always got high marks, especially in languages. He enjoyed playing soccer, and "Lolek the Goalie" played on both the Catholic and the Jewish teams. A natural leader, he was quickly put in charge of the altar boys and started a chapter of a religious youth group. He seemed to be able to get along with everyone, both children and adults.

Just before Karol turned nine, his mother died after a long illness. Although he knew she had been very ill for a long time, it was still a painful loss. Edmund's graduation from medical school and assignment to a nearby hospital made it easier to adjust. However, Edmund died in 1932 from scarlet fever, which he had contracted from a patient. Karol and his father were devastated. Prayer became their comfort.

At Marcin Wadowita State Secondary School, Karol discovered the world of theater. He joined the Drama Circle and played the starring role in several productions. He quickly earned a reputation as the best actor in Wadowice. His ability to memorize lines was legendary. On one occasion, he stepped in for another actor with only two days' notice and played both the new role and his own role perfectly. At the age of sixteen, he was hired by Mieczyslaw Kotlarczyk, director of a professional theater troupe. Karol felt that he had found his career.

He graduated from high school, ranking first in his class. After hearing him speak, Archbishop Adam Stefan Sapieha, Krakow's highest Catholic cleric, asked the local parish priest about Karol's career plans.

A young Karol Wojtyla is dressed for his role in a school play. The actress, writer, and traveler, Halina Krolikiewiczowna is pictured on his left.

Certain that Karol would make a good priest, Sapieha commented that "we could do with someone like that in the church." Told that Karol wanted to go into the theater, the archbishop replied, "A pity."

THE DOCUMENT

After his graduation, Karol and his father moved to a basement apartment in Krakow. Friends called it the catacombs, after the underground tombs of the early Christians. Karol attended Jagiellonian University in Krakow, where he studied the Polish language, literature, and theater.

However, his studies would soon come to an end. The dictator Adolf Hitler ruled Germany, Poland's neighbor to the west. In September 1939, Hitler's Nazi troops invaded Poland. This invasion marked the beginning of World War II (1939–1945). The Nazis

Mystics

In 1940, Karol met Jan Tyranowski, a mystic. Karol was fascinated and began to meet with members of a Living Rosary group that was studying mysticism. There have been many people in the Catholic Church who have identified themselves as mystics. Many still do so today. However, not all mystics are Catholic. A mystic is a person who sees his or her relationship with God personally. Mystics believe in God not because of the teachings of any church, but because they feel they know God. There have been many famous mystics over time, and some of them, such as Francis of Assisi, are now revered as saints by the Catholic Church.

promptly shut down the university. Professors were invited to a meeting, and those who attended were shipped off to concentration camps. Karol and his friends made a determined effort to keep Polish culture alive. They secretly continued their coursework, especially their theater work, in spite of the constant threat of execution or deportation to the concentration camps.

On February 18, 1941, Karol arrived home from getting medicine for his father to find the older man dead. Just twenty years old, Karol had now lost his entire family. What was worse, from his perspective, was that he had not been there with any of his family members when they had died. He turned to a deeper reliance on his faith to deal with his loss. For the first time, he considered the religious life—perhaps the austere, prayerful life of a Carmelite monk.

In addition to his underground studies and acting, Karol worked as a laborer under the Nazi occupation. Residents who were not working to support the war risked being sent to concentration camps. Karol was able to obtain work at the Solvay

Karol Sr. worked to develop discipline and a commitment to the church in his son. He told his son, "I will not live long and would like to be certain before I die that you will commit yourself to God's service."

chemical plant. He labored in their quarry, breaking up rocks that would provide material for explosives. The work was brutal and the food rations were meager. Working at temperatures well below zero, he put grease on his face to prevent frostbite. After three months in the quarry, he was able to switch to an indoor job, lugging the heavy pails of chemicals used to treat the plant's water supply.

In the fall of 1942, Karol decided to become a priest. The Nazis had shut down the seminaries, where young men study for the priesthood, so Karol had to study in secret. Of course, he also had to continue his work at Solvay, along with his university studies. In February 1944, as he walked home from a double shift at the factory, he was struck by a German army truck. Covered in blood, he was left for dead. Fortunately, a stranger found him and got him to a hospital for treatment.

On August 6, 1944, called Black Sunday, German occupiers went house to house rounding up all healthy males. They hoped to prevent a repeat of the uprising that had occurred in Warsaw, Poland's capital city, the previous week. The "catacombs" saved Karol that day, as the Germans didn't think the basement was habitable. In addition, the Gestapo (the Nazi secret police) arrested seven thousand priests, since they were seen as inciting rebellion among their parishioners.

A friend sneaked Karol into the archbishop's residence. There, wearing the long, black cassock of an ordained priest, he began his seminary studies full-time. On November 1, 1946, he was ordained a priest by Archbishop Sapieha, who had been so impressed by the young man years before. The archbishop must have been happy that, after surviving the rigors of the Nazi occupation, Karol had found his calling in the church.

Karol Wojtyla began his priesthood as a student in Rome, the world center of the Catholic Church. There he attended the Angelicum, a university run by the Dominican religious order. In 1948, he completed his doctoral studies in theology, the study of God and religion. Having lived in a Poland oppressed by Nazi Germany, he returned to a Poland oppressed by the communists of the Soviet Union, to the east. Both invading powers were totalitarian regimes, wielding absolute control. The two occupations by neighboring countries earned Poland a dubious honor: World War II was called "the war Poland lost twice."

Wojtyla's first assignment as a priest was to serve as an assistant pastor in the rural parish of Niegowic. He arrived in the summer of 1948, skinny, poor, and dressed in tattered clothing. He had so little money that he hadn't been able to afford to have his doctoral thesis from the Angelicum printed. His parishioners took pity on Wojtyla and gathered bedding for him. He promptly passed the bedding on to a woman who had been robbed. It was an indication of Wojtyla's unique style as a priest.

His listening skills were extraordinary and made him a cherished confidant who would spend hours with each parishioner. That level of attention meant he was always late, but he made up the lost time with an

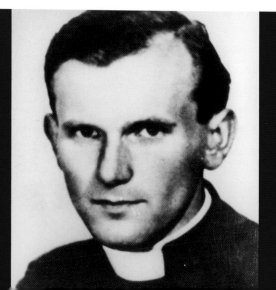

Before beginning his priestly duties in 1949, Karol was an avid student. In the three years between 1946 (when he was ordained) and 1949, he earned a master's degree and two doctorates.

amazing ability to listen while working on something else. He could lead a discussion group while answering his mail and still be able to summarize the entire discussion accurately. Wojtyla cared little for material possessions. Many years later, after he had become an archbishop, he was held by the police at a mountain checkpoint. The police officer was convinced he had stolen his credentials, as no archbishop would wear clothes in such poor condition.

After eight months in Niegowic, Wojtyla was reassigned as a chaplain to students at St. Florian's Church in Krakow. The students flocked to hear him speak and, under his guidance, soon formed a secret group known as the Srodowisko. The group would gather for intellectual dis-

Nazism and Communism

Nazism and communism were two prominent ideologies in the twentieth century. Although based on very different political philosophies, both were fundamentally opposed to the concept of individual human liberty. Nazism, the ideology that led to the outbreak of World War II in Europe, proposed a strong totalitarian state as the only way to protect society from undesirable persons and ideas. There was a strong emphasis on the persecution of non-Aryan races, which led directly to the mass extermination of Jews during the Holocaust. Communism, on the other hand, proposed control of the state by the people, organized as collectives and sharing everything in common. In practice, however, communism rapidly manifested itself as a totalitarian regime under an all-powerful Communist Party, which controlled all aspects of people's lives.

cussions and Masses, or Catholic worship services. They also took hiking, kayaking, and skiing trips. When camping, Wojtyla would say a secret Mass each morning using an overturned kayak as an altar, with paddles strapped together to form a cross. Priests were forbidden to organize youth groups, so the students called him Wujek, which means "uncle," to hide his identity. The nickname stuck.

Wojtyla was so devoted to his youth group that he continued meeting with them when he was sent to Jagiellonian University in 1951 to study for a doctorate in philosophy. As he was a new professor, students packed his classes in ethics and philosophy there and later at the Catholic University of Lublin. In 1956, when he was only thirty-six years old, he was appointed to the Chair of Ethics, an honored professorship, at Lublin. Wojtyla began publishing essays and poetry in the independent Catholic newspaper *Tygodnik Powszechny*, often under the pseudonym of Andrzej Jawien. He also authored several books on philosophy, the first published in 1960.

THE DIRT

As symbolized by the dirt buried with him, Karol Wojtyla had a lifelong dedication to Poland and its welfare. On July 4, 1958, he was appointed as bishop, the youngest in Poland's history. Then on December 30, 1963, he was appointed archbishop of Krakow. This was ironic in light of the intervention of the Polish Communist Party, his longtime adversary.

Party leaders wanted the new Krakow archbishop to be young, inexperienced, and nonpolitical so they could manipulate him to create division within the church. The party required the church to submit a list of names for approval as archbishop. The task of compiling this list fell to Cardinal Wyszynski, head of the Catholic Church in Poland and an ardent opponent of the communists. (Cardinals are high church officials, ranking just below the pope.) After a year and a half of rejecting candidates, the communists finally accepted Wyszynski's seventh choice—Karol Wojtyla. They could not have made a bigger mistake.

The archbishop of Krakow is traditionally seen as *defensor civitatis* ("defender of the city"), the protector of Krakow. Wojtyla took this role very seriously. He mastered the art of passive, unified resistance. When the party created the workers' town of Nowa Huta without a church, Karol celebrated Christmas Eve Mass there every year in an open field. Finally in 1967, the government allowed the construction of a church there. In 1964, he held the first ecumenical (multifaith) service in Krakow to help unite people of all faiths in resisting communism. He also ran an underground seminary for Catholics in Czechoslovakia, smuggling seminarians and supplies across the border.

Wojtyla recognized the need for church unity against the communist regime. He made this clear some years later, after he had become a cardinal. When Cardinal Wyszynski was denied a permit to go to Rome for a conference, Wojtyla showed his solidarity by declining his own invitation. Then the party approached Wojtyla and said they would allow him to build a new church if he would say just one critical thing about Wyszynski, but he refused. His support for Wyszynski even carried over into his humor. At a meeting with Italian cardinals, Wojtyla asked around to find someone who might go skiing with him. Told that Italian cardinals did not ski, he replied that 40 percent of Polish cardinals skied. When his puzzled companions pointed out that there were only two

Polish cardinals, Wojtyla answered that Wyszynski counted for 60 percent. He was making sure that the Italian cardinals knew that Wyszynski, not he, was the more important Polish cardinal.

Wojtyla's commitment to the welfare of the church extended beyond Poland. At the Second Vatican Council (1962–1965), a meeting of bishops from around the world, he lobbied for greater involvement in the church for laypeople, or those not in the clergy or religious orders. He also emphasized the need to work with non-Catholics to address world issues such as religious freedom. Pope Paul VI took notice of Wojtyla's growing influence and on June 26, 1967, made Wojtyla a cardinal. In 1971, he was elected to the church's prestigious Synod Council. This international committee of bishops organizes discussions of important church issues. In 1976, he was given the honor of leading the Lenten retreat—a period of prayer and meditation before Easter—for the pope and a select group of cardinals. Two years later, he was elected pope.

At the end of Wojtyla's life, all he did was reflected in those three focal points of the world's attention at his funeral—the man, the document of his life's work, and the dirt from his homeland. He was the actor, laborer, and outdoor adventurer—with experiences that enabled him to understand the needs of ordinary Catholics. He believed in learning, the pursuit of the truth, and the power of words based on core Catholic beliefs to overcome all challenges. His life showed an unceasing commitment to Poland and to all nations and peoples that are repressed or divided.

Cardinal Luciani wrote letters to literary and historical figures before being elected Pope John Paul I. *Illustrissimi* includes letters to Jesus Christ, Charles Dickens, Mark Twain, and Sir Walter Scott.

The First Polish Pope

The year 1978 is sometimes called the Year of Three Popes. Pope Paul VI, born Giovanni Battista Montini, died on August 6, 1978, after fifteen years as pope. He was the former archbishop of Milan, Italy, and speculation revolved around which Italian cardinal would succeed him as head of the Catholic Church. Although he was a cardinal, Karol Wojtyla would not have even come under serious consideration. For one thing, he was too young. Secondly, he was not Italian, and few people really felt it was possible to elect someone other than an Italian as pope. And the most important thing was that he was not an insider. That is, he was not one of the powerful cardinals who worked in the Vatican, the church's headquarters. But this would not be an ordinary year for the papacy.

Papal Terms

There are some terms that are used only when talking of popes, and some only upon the death of a pope. Among them are:

camerlengo—a church official who watches over papal property and money until the new pope is elected

conclave—a meeting of cardinals to elect a pope; it comes from the Latin words meaning "with a key," since the doors are closed to protect the secrecy of the proceedings

papabili—the possible popes, those most likely to be elected in the opinion of some students of the papacy; this is not a church phrase but one that came from the Italian media

habemus papam—Latin for "we have a pope"; the phrase everyone waits to hear to announce a new pope's election

papacy—the office of pope; also the term of a pope's reign

pontiff—another name for the pope; it comes from the Latin words for "bridge maker"

POPE OF SMILES

When the cardinals met to elect the new pope, they chose quickly. On August 26, 1978, the second day of the conclave, Cardinal Albino Luciani, archbishop of Venice, was elected pope after only four ballots. The first pope ever to have a double name, he chose the name Pope John Paul I to honor both of his predecessors—John XXIII and Paul VI. He quickly earned the nickname "the Pope of Smiles" for his friendliness. For the first time, the papacy moved away from using the royal "we" when he insisted on referring to himself as "I." He refused the more formal papal corona-tion in favor of a simple installation Mass. Everything about him seemed to prove that he would make a warm, pastorlike pope. Others speculated that he would not be able to handle the immense challenges associated with one of the most difficult jobs on earth.

However, he was pope for only a little over a month. He died in his sleep of an apparent heart attack or embolism (blood clot) on September 28, 1978. Although he was known to have health problems, his death led to many conspiracy theories about his being murdered. These theories reflected the absolute shock felt around the world when he died so soon after his election. Just as everyone was speculating about what decisions he would make and what impact he would have on the world, he was gone.

As the cardinals traveled to Rome to bury yet another pope and elect yet another cardinal to replace him, speculation centered on the two Italian cardinals said to be the strongest candidates—Cardinals Giuseppe Siri and Giovanni Benelli. There was equally strong specula-tion that the new pope would be someone other than the favorites, someone with the same warmth that John Paul I had conveyed in his short time as pope. There was also talk about the possibility of selecting a non-Italian for the papacy.

The story is told that it was Pope John Paul I who first predicted who would succeed him. Supposedly he told his secretary, Father John Magee, that he had sat facing the next pope in the Sistine Chapel during the conclave that elected him. When Magee later checked the seating chart for the first day of the conclave, he found that Pope John Paul I had indeed sat facing Cardinal Karol Wojtyla.

As for Cardinal Wojtyla himself, almost everyone who knew him well suspected that he might be chosen this time around. This wasn't based on any inside information, only on his outstanding talents. Many of Wojtyla's friends feared this outcome. It was not for lack of confidence in his considerable abilities. It was simply that they knew the intense pressures that popes were subjected to. And they knew Wojtyla did not want to be pope. Catholics in Poland also feared for themselves. They knew that, if their beloved countryman were elected, they would lose him to the world.

POPE WHO?

Conclaves are held in secret, so it is hard to piece together what happened in the conclave that elected Karol Wojtyla. It seems that the Italian favorites tried hard to defeat each other, causing a division among the cardinals that could not be reconciled in favor of either man. It also seems that Wojtyla, the compromise candidate whom everyone could support, did not much want the job. Inside accounts speak of Wojtyla quietly reading a philosophical journal as the voting went on. As the number of votes for him grew during the three days of the conclave, he put the book aside and appeared increasingly unhappy. Those who wanted him elected pope encouraged Cardinal Wyszynski to speak with him since, as one writer noted, "Wojtyla had learned long before that it was fruitless to argue with Wyszynski."

On the eighth ballot, the outcome was no longer in doubt. Only seventy-five votes were needed to elect him. He had received more than ninety. Karol Wojtyla was the new pope. Some cardinals who were there reported that he wept at the news. He changed into the white cassock awaiting him, accepted the allegiance of the cardinals, and headed toward his first encounter with the waiting world as the new pope. It was October 16, 1978.

As Cardinal Pericle Felici started the traditional ritual announcement of "*Habemus papam*," the crowd cheered each line and then waited in silence. When he finished announcing the name, there was no cheer—only a puzzled silence and then the murmur of voices asking, "*Chi è?*"—Who? For the people waiting for their new pope,

Former Polish Cardinal Karol Wojtyla appears as the newly elected Pope John Paul II on October 16, 1978. He is standing on the balcony overlooking St. Peter's Square in Vatican City.

knowing the name was no help. They did not know who this new pope was. Questions were shouted out, asking if he were black or Asian. The crowd was not pleased. This was an Italian crowd. Popes, to them, were supposed to be Italian. Not only was this pope not Italian, but they had no idea who he was. It would take a special man to win them over.

Pope John Paul II stepped out onto the balcony and began his papacy by breaking tradition. Before giving the traditional blessing, he addressed the confused crowd for a few moments. He spoke to them in Italian. He admitted that he was afraid to become pope but felt he must obey the will of God. He encouraged them to correct him if he didn't speak their language properly. It was enough to win them over. In just a few sentences, he captured their affection and their support. The crowd cheered.

Papal Nationalities

John Paul II was the only Polish pope, and Benedict XVI is only the sixth German pope, in the nearly two-thousand-year history of the papacy. The overwhelming majority of popes (more than 200 of the 265 popes to date) have been Italian—either ethnically Italian or from regions that later became part of Italy, such as Venice, Genoa, Naples, and Sicily. There have also been more than a dozen popes each from France and Greece. Others have come from Spain, Portugal, England, Belgium, Africa, and Dalmatia, a region in Croatia.

THE POLISH POPE

From the very beginning, everyone knew that it would not be business as usual in the Vatican. Here was a pope who was young, dynamic, and not an insider. Here was a pope with enormous presence, a pope who led others by the power of his voice. Here was a pope whose interests were not contained within the confines of the Vatican. Rather, he would engage the papacy in the politics and drama of the world. Here was a pope who was an actor, who knew the power of the media, and who would use it to make Catholicism felt throughout the world. From the moment the new pope took office, there was a strong sense that nothing would ever be the same again in the Vatican.

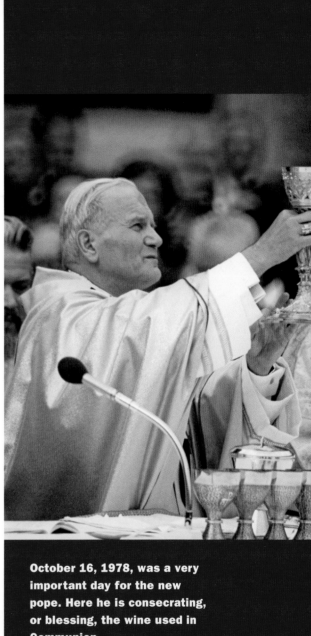

October 16, 1978, was a very important day for the new pope. Here he is consecrating, or blessing, the wine used in Communion.

The Second Vatican Council met in St. Peter's in Vatican City in 1962. This ecumenical council was instituted by Pope John XXIII (1958–1963).

THREE

John Paul II and the Church

Karol Wojtyla, as Pope John Paul II, would have had a great impact on the Catholic Church no matter what decisions he made, simply by virtue of the length of his papacy. He would also have had a strong impact on the church by virtue of his strong personality. Beyond that, he became pope at a time of great changes in the Catholic Church and in the world. Directives of the Second Vatican Council were having positive and negative effects in the church. The world itself was changing rapidly, with the development of new avenues of communication and transportation. Scientific knowledge was exploding and raising moral issues that would have been unthinkable a generation before. There was chaos politically, as the communist Soviet Union desperately tried to maintain its control of Eastern Europe.

THE SECOND VATICAN COUNCIL

Pope John Paul II began his papacy as the Catholic Church was still absorbing the enormous impact of the Second Vatican Council, often referred to as Vatican II. Vatican councils are rare meetings of all the world's bishops. The previous one had convened in 1869. Vatican II was called by Pope John XXIII, who said, "I want to throw open the windows of the Church so that we can see out and the people can see in."

Meeting in a series of sessions from 1962 to 1965, Vatican II resulted in major changes in the church, especially in terms of liturgy, or rites for public worship. The Mass would no longer be said in Latin throughout the world, but rather in the local language, making the worshipers more involved in the service. Laypeople would also have a

Papal Time

How long is a papacy? Pope John Paul II was the third-longest-serving pontiff. Only Saint Peter, the first head of the church (between thirty-four and thirty-seven years), and Pope Pius IX (thirty-one years) served longer. During John Paul II's twenty-six years as pope, the following U.S. presidents held office:

Jimmy Carter	1977–1981
Ronald Reagan	1981–1989
George H. W. Bush	1989–1993
William J. Clinton	1993–2001
George W. Bush	2001–

much stronger role in local church decisions and in parts of the liturgy.

Vatican II strengthened bishops' powers to govern their dioceses, or territories. It also gave bishops a greater opportunity to take part in church decisions through a new Synod of Bishops that met regularly. Members of religious orders were freed from regulations about wearing their traditional religious clothing and were given additional roles in the church.

Another major theme that emerged from Vatican II was ecumenism, a spirit of unity and cooperation among the religions of the world. One document from the council, for example, reaffirmed that Jews were not responsible for the death of Christ and called for a rejection of anti-Semitism throughout the world. Vatican II also moved toward healing the split between the Roman Catholic Church and the Eastern Orthodox Church, a division that had lasted for almost a thousand years. All these innovations

Pope John Paul II was a pope of the people. In 1983, he baptized twenty newborn children in the Sistine Chapel in Vatican City.

challenged and weakened the power of the Curia, the administrative offices of the church.

Karol Wojtyla was an active participant in Vatican II and was seen as a reformer who supported the council's changes. He was also known as a strong proponent of ecumenism and of the need for the church to play an active role in international issues such as human rights. Now he would have the chance to put his mark on all the changes taking place as a result of Vatican II.

"BE NOT AFRAID"

Karol Wojtyla had taken as his personal motto "Be Not Afraid." He would need it in the days ahead of him. Immediately after donning the white papal robes, the new pope met with his cardinals, who knelt before him in the Sistine Chapel. This pope chose to stand rather than sit, as previous popes had, to receive their pledges of support. A small change, perhaps, but

More than thirty thousand people attended this general audience in St. Peter's Square on March 29, 1989. John Paul II knew how to work a crowd, making everyone happy to be there.

it was an indication of how this pope would govern. From the first moments of his papacy, the new pontiff was truly in charge of the church.

In his first address to Catholics the day after his election, John Paul II began to sound the themes that the church would hear for his entire papacy. He voiced strong support for Vatican II, but he also made clear that he would carry out the council's decisions with an "appropriate mentality" and in a way that was "prudent." He also pledged to "preserve intact the deposit of faith" in the face of "the attacks which in our time are being leveled here and there against certain truths of the Catholic faith." John Paul II's papacy would take a combination of directions, changing some traditions and preserving others.

Traditionally, when a pope is inaugurated, an ornate papal crown is placed on his head as a sign of his authority. Pope John Paul I had declined to wear this crown, and so did his successor. John Paul II said he had refused the crown because it was a symbol that no longer represented the church. A new papal coat of arms is traditionally designed for each new pope. However, this pope declined that tradition as well, insisting on keeping the coat of arms he had had as bishop of Krakow. At the same time, he took seriously the pope's traditional role as bishop of Rome, visiting the various churches around Rome and becoming involved in their day-to-day decisions.

The new pope also made sure that he controlled developments within the church. On the one hand, he claimed to support a collegial model of church governance—one in which bishops were involved in the decision-making process. This had been a prominent theme in Vatican II. At the same time, however, he made clear that he was in charge. Bishops might offer advice and input, but he made the decisions.

Pope John Paul II traveled to Mexico in January 1999. Millions of people flocked to get a glimpse of him either in his Popemobile or at a podium.

FOUR

John Paul II, the Pope of the World

Pope John Paul II would become a large presence on the world stage. The actor Karol Wojtyla found in the papacy a forum large enough to allow him to bring about real change. He would use the moral force of the papacy as a tool in international politics. He would use it to further his long-held views on ecumenism and on the need for healing among all religions. He would travel extensively and take his message to the millions who would see and receive him. He would be the first pope to make the world his pulpit.

COMMUNISM

Wojtyla had long been an enemy of communism. As pope, he was able to contribute to dissent within communist nations. Poland, the pope's homeland, became a special focus for him. There, he used his moral authority to encourage the move toward peaceful revolt.

He began with a nine-day trip to Poland in June 1979. As the massive crowds enthusiastically welcomed their pope, he avoided overt attacks on Poland's communist regime. At the same time, his presence and the knowledge of how he had fought the communists in the past sent a resounding message through the Polish people. Their pride in their pope gave them a level of hope that had long been missing. His pilgrimage through Poland, beginning as all his trips did, by his kissing the ground, was officially for religious reasons. No one was fooled, however. His presence alone said that this trip also served a political purpose.

He returned again in June 1983, when Poland's movement toward freedom seemed to be losing ground. Now he acted the defensor civitatis

On June 6, 1979, the pope celebrated Mass in Victory Square in Warsaw, Poland. Large, adoring crowds met him wherever he went during nine days in his home country.

that he had been as archbishop of Krakow. His real impact was on the faith of the Poles, a faith that was enhanced by seeing one of their own become pope. That strength of faith gave them hope when there seemed to be none.

After John Paul II's death, former Soviet leader Mikhail Gorbachev reminisced about the pope, whom he felt had helped bring about the collapse of communism. When they had talked, Gorbachev said, the pope had been "very, very critical of communism." After his death, one news source called him a "geopolitician of the first rank."

ECUMENISM

From his first address on the day after his election, John Paul II spoke of ecumenism as an issue that was important to him. This was no surprise. After all, as "Lolek the Goalie," he had often played soccer on a Jewish team. As archbishop, he had organized an ecumenical prayer service to encourage people of all faiths to work together to resist communism in Poland. That emphasis on ecumenism would last throughout his papacy. It was most evident in his encyclical *Ut Unum Sint*, issued on May 25, 1995: "My earnest desire is to renew this call today, to propose it once more with determination, repeating what I said at the Roman Coliseum on Good Friday 1994 . . . that believers in Christ, united in following in the footsteps of the martyrs, cannot remain divided."

This pope put his words into action. He was the first pope to participate in a prayer service at Canterbury Cathedral with an Anglican archbishop. In 1533, the Anglican Church had broken away from the Catholic Church because King Henry VIII of England wanted to get divorced.

Now the pope was worshiping with the Anglican leader. It was a momentous statement of his desire to reconcile differences between the two churches.

In December 1983, he continued his spirit of goodwill toward Protestants, this time preaching at a Lutheran church. However, he also reached out to those who were not Christian. In 1986, when he arranged a World Day of Prayer in Assisi, Italy, he invited 150 non-Catholic religious leaders to attend. African animists (believers in spirits in the world of nature) joined the group, along with tribal shamans and Hindu holy men. Each leader voiced his prayer for peace. Pope John Paul II summed up the importance of the event: "Diversity is the nature of the human family. . . . We must go beyond [Catholicism] to persons of goodwill who do not share our faith."

He also attempted to find common ground on certain moral issues with the followers of Islam. In May 2001, on a visit to Syria, he became the first pope ever to visit a Muslim mosque. He made friends with people of all faiths, meeting several times with the Buddhist leader, the Dalai Lama, who shared his views on the dangers of totalitarian governments.

His most determined ecumenical effort was his attempt to heal the Great Schism, or split, between the Roman Catholic Church and the Eastern Orthodox Church. The pope met and prayed with the patriarch of Constantinople, the highest Eastern Orthodox official. He made several other attempts to resolve differences between the two churches.

In his outreach to Jews, Pope John Paul II made a striking impression. He became the first pope since Saint Peter to pray in a synagogue. He was also the first pope to visit a Nazi concentration camp when he went to Auschwitz, not far from his former home in Poland. There, only eight months after becoming pope, he prayed at a memorial for the Jews killed at the camp, noting that "It is not permissible for anyone to pass by this [place] with indifference."

In a visit to Israel in 2000, he was not afraid to apologize for past anti-Semitism in the Catholic Church. In a ceremony at the Western Wall in Jerusalem, he, like countless pilgrims before him, placed a prayer in a crack in the wall. His read, "We are deeply saddened by the behavior of those who in the course of history have caused these children of yours to suffer, and asking your forgiveness we wish to commit ourselves to genuine brotherhood with the people of the Covenant."

THE TRAVELING POPE

The numbers are mind numbing, even for a twenty-six year papacy. Pope John Paul II visited 129 countries and has been called the most recognized person in the world. He was everywhere. The pictures were the same from country to country—of enormous, cheering crowds and of him, after exiting his plane, kneeling and kissing the ground. Through this symbolic gesture, he showed his belief that God was in each of these places and with each of these people.

The visits began three months into his papacy and over the years led to an almost limitless number of firsts. He was the first pope to ride on a Concorde jet. He was the first pope to visit Ireland and the first to visit Scandinavia. He visited Japan and addressed the parliament in Japanese (and then stopped off in Alaska on the way back to go dogsledding). He made several trips to Africa and even donned a native headdress for ceremonies there.

On a visit to Seoul, South Korea, in 1984, he canonized 103 Korean saints. (Canonization is the process by which the church officially declares someone a saint after death.) This was the first time any canonizations had taken place outside of Rome since the Middle Ages. He visited the Pacific island of Guam and spoke to the natives in their own language. In the Philippines, he addressed a gathering of more than five million people. This is thought to be the largest group of people gathered together in all of human history.

When he traveled to meet with political leaders and heads of state, he refused to let them ride with him in the Popemobile. Because he came as a representative of the church, only church leaders could ride with him.

The Popemobile

Everywhere that Pope John Paul II went in his travels, his Popemobile went with him. This vehicle (there were several of them over the course of his papacy) allowed him to be seen and to travel through crowds in safety. The vehicle had bulletproof glass to protect him from assassination attempts, like the one in which he was seriously injured on May 13, 1981, and as his suffering from Parkinson's disease increased, the Popemobile allowed him a measure of comfort on his extensive travels. After the election of Pope Benedict XVI, everyone watched to see whether there would be a new Popemobile. On the day of his installation, the new pope rode around the crowds in St. Peter's Square in a new vehicle with an open top. There is a separate papal airplane, as well. The pope travels on a plane nicknamed Shepherd One, operated by Alitalia, the Italian national airline.

However, reporters who traveled on the papal airplane, Shepherd One, tell of the pope mingling with them and holding impromptu news conferences, answering the reporters in their own languages.

In 1995, Pope John Paul II addressed the United Nations, insisting that "The quest for freedom cannot be suppressed." He visited the United States seven times, and in 1979 he became the first pope ever to visit the White House.

His travels brought him into contact with leaders of countries throughout the world. More important, he used that contact to speak for people who often were not heard by those in power. Pope John Paul II made a special point of visiting native peoples whose needs were often ignored by modern society. He made himself their champion and, indeed, the champion of all those he felt were deprived of basic human rights and freedoms.

This pope never hesitated to take both of the major superpowers, the Soviet Union and the United States, to task for the way they governed. He took a firm stand against communism. Yet, he was equally disappointed in capitalism, with goods produced in a free market rather than under government control. He saw democracy as a worthy goal for the world, while denouncing the worldly, nonreligious outlook that seemed to accompany democracy in the West.

After his death, some news organizations reported that he had traveled one out of every ten days of his papacy. He had covered 725,000 miles (1,167,000 kilometers) in his journeys, the equivalent of traveling to the Moon three times. Surveys showed that he was the single most recognized person on earth by the time he died. He had revolutionized the papacy, making it a force to be reckoned with and a symbol of human dignity in the farthest corners of the world. It was indeed a large stage, but the actor Karol Wojtyla had made it his own.

Before using a Popemobile with bulletproof glass, the pope rode through crowds in an open-top vehicle. On May 13, 1981, Pope John Paul II was shot twice in an assassination attempt while greeting people in St. Peter's Square.

FIVE

The Human Pope Meets Death

In 1979, less than a year into his papacy, John Paul II began construction on a swimming pool at the papal summer residence at Castel Gandolfo. When some questioned the cost, he quipped that he needed the exercise and that it was less expensive than holding another conclave.

Popes serve for life. Because most popes are quite old when they are elected, they do not generally serve for a long period of time. Wojtyla was only fifty-eight when he became pope, and he was the picture of vigor and health. Over the twenty-six years of his papacy, the world would see the vigorous man fade, become stooped, and, at the end, lose his voice. His mind would remain sharp, but his body would betray him.

Pope John Paul II prays in St. Peter's Basilica at the Vatican. He presided over Mass on January 1, 2005.

year to join him at the Vatican. He entertained them and participated in all the festivities and in a large Mass. He also wrote a memoir for the occasion, *Gift and Mystery*, recalling the process of his decision to become a priest.

The pope remained active until just a few months before his death. Even to the last, he tried to continue his ministry to his people, sometimes visibly frustrated when he failed. By the end of his papacy, he had produced an enormous number of formal writings—totaling close to one hundred thousand pages—on all aspects of the church. He had visited more than half the countries of the world, many several times. He also canonized more saints than any previous pope, recognizing holy people from a variety of cultures spanning the globe.

THE FINAL MONTHS

In the spring of 2005, his physical infirmities became too much for the frail, eighty-four-year-old pontiff. First, a flu in February led to breathing difficulties and a stay at the Policlinico Gemelli. He returned to the Vatican, only to be admitted again. This time it was for a tracheotomy, a surgery to open his windpipe and ease his breathing. Again back in the papal apartment, he tried to resume his duties. It seemed that every time he appeared to be gaining strength, he would suffer another setback. On March 30, doctors inserted a feeding tube so he could receive additional nourishment.

Then on the night of March 31, the pope became gravely ill. The world began a deathwatch, while sixty thousand people prayed for him in St. Peter's Square. It ended at 9:37 P.M. Rome time on April 2. His secretary and others were with him in the hours before he died. They say that he remained alert until the very end. He was aware of the crowds praying for him and was touched by their devotion.

Archbishop Leonardo Sandri announced the death to the waiting world: "Our most beloved Holy Father John Paul II returned to the house of the Father. Let us pray for him." Although the death was expected, world reaction was surprising in its intensity. It became clear that this pope had been a widely honored figure, a shepherd to Catholic and non-Catholic alike. His impact could be seen in the long lines of mourners who came to pay their respects as his body lay in state in St. Peter's Basilica. By some estimates, the mourners may have numbered as many as four million. The funeral to follow would be the largest one in the history of the papacy and, many believe, the largest funeral ever held in world history.

THE FUNERAL

On April 8, 2005, Karol Wojtyla's journey came to an end when his cypress coffin was enclosed inside two others and lowered into the crypt below St. Peter's Basilica. The scene in the hours before that simple, private ceremony was of historic proportions. Leading the Requiem Mass, or funeral Mass, was Cardinal Joseph Ratzinger. He was dean of the College of Cardinals, the assembly of all the cardinals in the church. Concelebrating, or jointly officiating in the Mass, were about 160 other cardinals, along with patriarchs of Eastern Rite Catholicism. Also in attendance was the archbishop of Canterbury, head of the Anglican Church, along with Jewish, Muslim, and various other Christian leaders.

Filling St. Peter's Square were heads of state from more than fifty countries, along with an estimated five hundred thousand people. Watching on television were another two billion people—about twice the number of Catholics in the entire world. The ceremony was a moving spectacle, filled with traditional symbolism and drama. It was also visually moving—the simple wood casket with the gospel pages moving in the

The Swiss Guard

Who are those guys in the colorful uniforms roaming around Vatican City? They are the Swiss Guards, the official guards responsible for the safety of all popes. Pope Julius II first hired 150 of them from Switzerland in 1506. Ever since then, new popes have continued to choose their guards from Switzerland. They are real soldiers, and when a German army sacked Rome in 1527, 147 of them died defending the pope. Their uniforms are said to have been designed by Michelangelo, the Renaissance artist, sculptor, and architect who was Pope Julius's artist in residence.

breeze, the bright colors of the cardinals' robes contrasting with the black mourning clothes of the attending world leaders, the colorful uniforms of the pope's Swiss Guard—a medieval pageant for a modern world.

This pageant was a catholic one in the nonreligious sense of the word—that is, "universal." It was, in fact, the world's largest-ever gathering of heads of state. One hundred and five countries sent representatives to the funeral. Official delegations were seated in alphabetical order by the French names of their countries. This produced some interesting neighbors in the various rows. President George W. Bush, the first American president to attend a papal funeral, was sitting close to the president of Iran, a frequent U.S. opponent. The presidents of Syria and Israel, longtime adversaries, sat close enough to shake hands. The president of Zimbabwe, forbidden to travel in European Union countries, shook hands with Prince Charles of Great Britain.

Cardinal Joseph Ratzinger gave a moving homily. Often he repeated the phrase "Follow me," which he said summarized the life of the late pope. "Our pope," he said, "wanted to give of himself unreservedly, to the very last moment." It was indeed a fitting eulogy for the man who brought the world to St. Peter's Square for one last visit.

People in the crowd repeatedly cried "*santo subito*"—"sainthood at once." It would come as no surprise that John Paul's successor, Pope Benedict XVI, responded to this sentiment. He announced in May 2005 that he was setting aside the requirement that five years must pass before the late pope could be considered for sainthood. This Polish pope, who had captivated the world in life, would be a difficult act for his successor to follow.

Archbishop Piero Marini closes the doors to the Sistine Chapel on April 18, 2005, for a conclave to elect a new pope. This centuries-old custom is immersed in secrecy.

SIX

How a New Papacy Is Born

People around the world know what to expect when leaders die. In countries ruled by kings or queens, leadership is predetermined by heredity. In totalitarian countries, the next leader is sure to come from a small, select group of candidates. Even in democracies, where a transfer of leadership does not usually take place because of death, the likely candidates are well known before election time.

When a new pope is to be chosen, however, the outcome is hard to predict. There is simply no sure way of knowing ahead of time who will emerge as the choice of the secret conclave of cardinals. In fact, the saying is, "He who goes into the conclave [thinking he is] a pope, comes out a cardinal." For all the guessing ahead of time, the decision takes place only after the doors close on the conclave in the Sistine

Chapel. There, church leaders say, they are guided by the Holy Spirit in determining what is best for the future of the church. It is an election system that has changed over the centuries but remains a secret and mysterious process. From it a new pope emerges, takes on a new name, and begins a new life.

HOW POPES HAVE BEEN ELECTED IN THE PAST

In a church with traditions dating back nearly two thousand years, it might seem that popes must have been chosen the same way since the beginning. But this is not true. In the first thousand years, the succession of popes was a very haphazard process at best. In fact, at one point, in the year 498, two separate groups of church leaders met in two different churches in Rome and elected two different popes. Theodoric the Ostrogoth, who had just conquered Italy, finally selected Symmachus as the pope in that election.

Many centuries would pass before a real set of rules emerged for electing a pope. In some cases, actual papal dynasties arose, with popes trying to ensure that relatives would succeed them. At other times, heads of nations would force the selection of a certain pope.

Finally in 1059, the College of Cardinals was given the official duty of electing the pope. Still, the college was filled with church leaders who were often chosen for their political connections to kings rather than for their devotion to the church. In 1274, it took a church council in Lyons, France, to decide that the electors should meet in secret. It wasn't until the 1400s that the Sistine Chapel was built, and it did not become the accepted place for all conclaves until 1870.

How Long Does It Take to Elect a Pope?

Modern popes are elected fairly quickly. Every pope since 1831 has been elected within five days of the start of the conclave. For all but three of these popes, it took fewer than ten ballots to select them. It was not always this way. When Pope Nicholas IV died on April 4, 1292, the conclave that began ten days later lasted for more than two years. The new pope, Celestine V, was not elected until July 5, 1294!

Over the years, some of the stories told about conclaves have been almost amusing. Pope Gregory X was elected pope in 1271 after the people locked up the arguing cardinals in the papal palace—and tore off its roof! Gregory X used this example to establish rules for how the cardinals would live during conclaves: They would be locked in a small area, they would have to share rooms and facilities, and their food allowances would be cut after three days of meetings. To encourage them still further to arrive at a decision, they would be fed only bread, water, and wine if the conclave lasted more than five days.

In the last one hundred years, traditions have developed that are still followed today. Elections take place in the Sistine Chapel. The conclave is secret, and the cardinals have no contact with the outside world once they enter the conclave. Ballots are burned after they are counted. If no pope has been chosen after a ballot, black smoke is sent through the chimney. If a pope has been elected, white smoke informs those outside. Still, each pope revises procedures for the election that will follow his death. John Paul II was no exception.

NEW RULES FOR ELECTING THE POPE

In 1996, Pope John Paul II delivered his plans for his successor's election in a document entitled *Universi Dominici Gregis* ("The Lord's Whole Flock"). Under his plans, the cardinals' living quarters would improve because the Vatican was building them a hotel within the grounds of Vatican City. The 130-room Domus Sanctae Marthae (Saint Martha's House) is not just for cardinals attending conclaves but also for visiting clergy. It has air-conditioning and private rooms with baths—a definite improvement over the days when cardinals slept in dormitories and ten cardinals shared a bath.

Many of John Paul II's changes had to do with procedures. The conclave would begin between fifteen and twenty days after the death of the pope. There would be no more than four ballots a day, and after three days there would be a day of prayer. This would be followed by seven more

The Sistine Chapel

The chapel where the College of Cardinals meets to elect a new pope is called the Sistine Chapel. It is named for Pope Sixtus IV (1471–1484), who had it built. It was designed specifically for papal elections and for other times when all the important church leaders would meet together. This pope's nephew and successor, Pope Julius II, arranged for the chapel's artwork. He commissioned the reluctant Michelangelo, who much preferred sculpture to painting, to paint *The Last Judgment* on the wall behind the altar and the magnificent biblical story on the ceiling of the chapel.

ballots (if necessary) and another day of prayer. After two more sets of seven ballots, if a pope had not been elected, a two-thirds majority would no longer be required and a new pope could be elected by a simple majority. John Paul II reaffirmed Pope Paul VI's ruling that only cardinals who were eighty years old or younger when the pope died could vote in the conclave. Of course, the one rule from the past that remained absolute was that of secrecy. The Sistine Chapel was even remodeled with a fake floor with the latest high-tech jamming equipment beneath it to prevent anyone from hearing what is happening inside.

One other change was welcomed by all those who could not tell the outcome of past papal elections, because the "white" smoke signaling the election of a pope came out gray. Now, after the white smoke signal, the bells of St. Peter's would ring to announce the news also.

THE NEW CARDINAL ELECTORS

John Paul II's long reign had a profound effect on the makeup of the College of Cardinals. One hundred and seventeen cardinals met the age requirements as cardinal electors. Two indicated they would not attend for health reasons. Of the remaining 115 cardinals, this conclave would be the first for all but two of them. The overwhelming majority of the men who would elect the next pope had been appointed by John Paul II. This meant that they generally supported his views. Because he had appointed cardinals from many countries, they represented an international viewpoint, rather than the Italian focus of the past. The world waited anxiously to see whom they would choose.

The Sistine Chapel was built between 1475 and 1483. It is the exact measurements of the Temple of Solomon given in the Old Testament of the Bible.

SEVEN

The Election

ecause Pope John Paul II had been the first non-Italian pope in more than four hundred years, the outcome of this conclave would be especially hard to predict. The changes in the College of Cardinals added to the widespread speculation about the papabili, or possible papal candidates. Few people would have predicted Karol Wojtyla's election in 1978, but that did not stop anyone from trying to predict who might be the likely choice this time. Discussions focused on three decisions the cardinal electors would be making. The first was whether they should elect an older, "caretaker" pope who would have a short papacy. The second was whether a pope would be selected from a Third World country for the first time. The third was whether the new papacy should be strongly conservative or more moderate in tone.

CARETAKER POPE VERSUS ACTIVIST POPE

Even before people began wondering who the next pope would be, there was talk about what kind of papacy the church needed at this point in history. After John Paul II's long reign, many felt that it might not be a good idea to select another young pope who might live for another twenty-five to thirty years. ("Young" by papal standards means late fifties to early sixties.) Many Vatican leaders felt that the church needed time to slow down and absorb all the changes that had taken place in John Paul II's twenty-six years as pope. Perhaps, it was felt, it might be good to elect someone already in his mid-seventies who would have a shorter reign. This pope would be a kind of caretaker who could focus on continuity and give controversial issues time to settle.

Those opposed to this position argued that the papacy had become too important a force in the world to have a caretaker pope. Under John Paul II, the papacy had made a worldwide impact. Many felt this impact would be lost if the new pope stepped back from an activist role. They also pointed out the last time someone who was meant to be a caretaker pope was chosen. It was in 1958, when Pope John XXIII was elected. This "seat-warming pope" proceeded to organize Vatican II. In less than five years as pope, he managed to create more change in the church than had occurred in more than a thousand years. The cardinals might intend to elect a caretaker pope, but that didn't mean they would get one. One observer quoted a famous Italian saying: "There is no one as dead as a dead pope." The point was that all popes, no matter how little they may be expected to do, set their own course once they are elected.

A POPE FROM THE WEST OR FROM THE THIRD WORLD?

Before John Paul II was elected, the whole discussion about papabili would have centered on which Italian cardinal would be the next pope. Just for novelty's sake, a few might speculate on the possibility of a non-Italian pope, but that was generally viewed as too unlikely to be serious. This time, anyone chosen from the West, the developed world, would be seen as the "traditional" selection. If a non-Westerner, someone from the Third World, were chosen, this would represent a radical change from the past. The excitement over the possibility of a pope coming from the Third World led to intense speculation.

There were still those who felt that the Italians might "take back" the papacy. Among the Italians, the most talked-about cardinal was the archbishop of Milan, Cardinal Dionigi Tettamanzi. Two younger cardi-

German cardinal Joseph Ratzinger and Italians Angelo Scola and Dionigi Tettamanzi were considered strong candidates for succeeding Pope John Paul II.

nals, Angelo Scola of Venice and Ennio Antonelli of Florence, were also mentioned as possible choices. Most of the speculation in the media, however, was that the Italians would not have a chance of reestablishing their long hold on the papacy. This was because they no longer had the voting numbers in the College of Cardinals that they once had.

Among other Europeans, many names were mentioned, but most of them were quickly dismissed after a few days of speculation. Cardinal Godfried Danneels of Belgium was on most of the early lists, but his health quickly relegated him to a less-likely choice. A Ukrainian cardinal, Lubomyr Husar, was mentioned as a possible choice, but the cardinals were not expected to elect another eastern European to follow a Polish pope. Austrian Christoph Schönborn was dismissed as much too young,

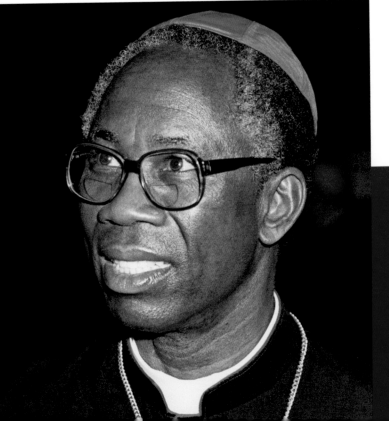

People speculated whether the pope would be chosen from a Third World country. Cardinal Francis Arinze, a Nigerian, is the president of the Vatican's Pontifical Council for inter-religious dialogue.

at only sixty years of age! One name kept coming up as the speculation continued. It was Joseph Ratzinger, the seventy-seven-year-old German cardinal who had celebrated the funeral Mass for Pope John Paul II.

From the very beginning, it was made clear that no American cardinals would be considered. There were two reasons for this. The first was that the American church was seen as too liberal for the rest of the world. That liberalism takes many forms. Partly, Americans are more liberal on social issues such as women's rights and workers' rights. Also, within the American church, there is a stronger belief in the authority of an individual's moral conscience and stronger support for more democratic governing structures within the church. A second reason for ruling out American cardinals was that the United States was already too powerful a presence in the world to have the power of the papacy as well. A Canadian cardinal, Marc Ouellet of Quebec City, made some of the lists that appeared on Internet news sites, but he wasn't seen as a serious contender. He, like Cardinal Schönborn, was considered too young at age sixty.

It was the possibility of a pope from a Third World country that really captured media attention. For the first time in history, some of the most popular candidates came from outside the traditional Western Catholic countries. Cardinals from Brazil, Argentina, Colombia, Nigeria, India, and Indonesia were all mentioned as papabili.

With more than 40 percent of the world's Catholics living in Latin America, it was not surprising that several Latin American cardinals were on various media lists of favorites. The leading candidate seemed to be Brazil's Cardinal Claudio Hummes, a priest from the Franciscan religious order, known for his support of workers in Brazil. Other cardinals from Latin America also brought on discussions about the role of the Catholic

Church in assisting the poor against governments that seemed to ignore their needs. Colombia's Dario Castrillón Hoyos made some lists because of his fight to defend poor Colombians caught in that country's drug wars. Argentina's Cardinal Jorge Mario Bergoglio was considered for his openness and compassion. Cardinals from Cuba, Mexico City, Honduras, and the Dominican Republic were also mentioned as papabili.

Indonesia's Cardinal Julius Darmaatmadja appeared on some lists. It was believed that, as pope, he could work well with Islamic nations. His expertise was well established, as Indonesia has the largest Muslim population in the world. India's Cardinal Ivan Dias was considered because of his diplomatic background. South Africa's Wilfrid Fox Napier was identified as a potential candidate for his strong support of collegiality, the practice of allowing bishops to have more regional control over their churches. The most media attention went to Cardinal Francis Arinze of Nigeria. Many believed he could become the first black pope. Arinze's personal leadership, his skill in dealing with other religious groups, and his conservatism on moral issues made him a favorite among the media as the conclave began.

A CONSERVATIVE OR A MODERATE?

The third deciding factor would be how conservative the various papabili would be. Only a few were seen as moderate, or open to change within the church. As Catholics around the world were interviewed, surveyed, and polled, it became clear that their opinions differed widely. Even in the United States, surveys showed that Catholics were divided on the direction the church was heading and the views the next pope should have.

All but three of the cardinal electors had been appointed by Pope John Paul II. So everyone knew the electors would choose a pope with conservative views on moral issues. The only question was about the degree of conservatism.

Cardinal Carlo Maria Martini, the retired archbishop of Milan, seemed to be the most open to change. Revered as a holy man, he is also a member of the Jesuit religious order and a great scholar. His position as a moderate made him stand out among the conservative papabili.

At the same time, people spoke of the danger of an ultraconservative. Here the name most often mentioned was that of Cardinal Ratzinger. Some observers viewed him as a divisive force. As head of the church's Congregation for the Doctrine of the Faith, he was strongly identified with the enforcement of church teachings. Some felt this made it impossible for him to unite all Catholics. It was not that other papabili would have disagreed with Cardinal Ratzinger on moral issues. Cardinal Arinze, for example, was seen as quite firm about morals. He had

Cardinal Carlo Maria Martini makes his last public appearance before the conclave begins. The cardinals who will elect a new pope meet in the Sistine Chapel and sleep and eat in private quarters nearby.

Papal Clothing

The new pope is presented to the world on the balcony of St. Peter's Basilica about an hour after he is elected. On the way to his presentation, he changes into the white vestments worn only by a pope. How does the Vatican have the right size ready for the new pope to wear? The Vatican orders the handmade garments in three sizes so that they will fit any of the cardinals. The vestments are made by a local tailor shop that has been run by the Gammarelli family since 1798.

angered many American Catholics with his statements about whether Catholic politicians who support abortion should be allowed to receive the Eucharist at Mass.

However, others besides Ratzinger were more likely to focus on social issues, such as inequities between the West and the Third World. Cardinals Hummes, Arinze, Bergoglio, and others were seen as having a vision that went beyond simply defending moral issues. They addressed the broader issues of social change and the role that the papacy might play in bringing about such change.

THE DOORS ARE CLOSED

On Monday, April 18, 2005, after days of frenzied speculation, the 115 cardinals prepared to enter the conclave to elect a new pope. According to press leaks from Italy, the front-runner was Cardinal Ratzinger. News accounts claimed that he had fifty of the seventy-seven votes needed to be elected pope. Cardinals Arinze, Hummes, and Tettamanzi, however, were all seen as strong contenders. Cardinal Ratzinger himself gave the homily at the Mass that opened the conclave, speaking strongly to the world about the dangers of "relativism—letting ourselves be carried away by any wind of doctrine . . . that leaves as the final standard only one's own ego and desires." The Mass completed, the cardinals filed into the Sistine Chapel to cast their votes. With the cry of "*Extra omnes*," Latin for "everyone out," the doors were closed. The next time the world saw the cardinals, one of them would be wearing the white vestments of a pope.

The new pope greets the crowd for the first time from the balcony of St. Peter's Basilica in the Vatican. Thousands of visitors waited many hours to get a glimpse of Pope Benedict XVI.

Pope Benedict XVI stands on the balcony with the crowd in St. Peter's Square below. Many thought he was too old to be elected pope.

EIGHT

Habemus Papam—We Have a Pope

The 265th pope, Benedict XVI, was elected on April 19, 2005, when Cardinal Joseph Ratzinger won the required two-thirds majority vote in the Sistine Chapel on the fourth ballot. As gray and then white smoke poured forth from the chimney of the Sistine Chapel, people watched eagerly and then cheered. They had already seen black smoke after the ballot the previous evening and after the two ballots taken that morning. A few minutes after the white smoke appeared, the bells began tolling, and the world knew that there was a new pope.

Everyone watched anxiously, cheers rising every time it appeared that the doors might open on the balcony where the new pope would appear in his white papal garments. After what seemed like an interminable wait, Cardinal Medina Estevez appeared and announced "*Habemus papam*"—"We have a pope." Pope Benedict XVI stepped forward on the balcony and addressed, and then blessed, his cheering flock. A new papacy had begun.

CHILDHOOD

Joseph Alois Ratzinger was born in Marktl am Inn, Germany, on April 16, 1927. This village is in Bavaria, in the southern part of Germany, not far from the Austrian border. The house where he was born still stands in the village. However, he did not grow up there. The family moved away when he was a small child. Despite having lived in many other places, he still visits the village. The townspeople are proud of their native son and excited that he has become pope. Villagers sometimes visit him, too. In 1998, he arranged for a group of people from the village who were visiting Rome to have dinner with him and then to meet Pope John Paul II.

Joseph was born on Holy Saturday, the day before Easter. He was baptized the same day with the newly blessed holy water from the Easter Vigil service. In his autobiography years later, he noted that "To be the first person baptized with the new water was seen as a significant act of Providence." This, he said, later influenced his decision to serve God in some way. Even at an early age, he knew this was his path in life. When he was five years old, a cardinal visited his town, and he was one of the children chosen to present flowers to their guest. Seeing the cardinal up close in his clerical vestments impressed young Joseph, who decided that day that he would like to be a cardinal.

Joseph's parents, Joseph and Maria Ratzinger, married in 1920 and had two other children by the time he was born—a daughter named Maria, born in 1921, and a son named Georg, born in 1924. His mother worked as a cook at local small hotels to help support the family. His father was a policeman who also opposed the Nazis, which meant the family had to move often. The moves did not change Ratzinger's memories of a happy childhood with his family, however. His father retired at age sixty, when Joseph was only nine years old. Since his father was no longer in the public eye, the family was able to stay in one location. They settled just outside of Traunstein in the village of Hufschlag, and from then on, Joseph would consider this area his home. He would later write that he inherited his "critical mind" from his father and a "warm-hearted religious sense" from his mother.

Papal Names

Early popes used their own names. Historians say that this tradition changed when a pope named Mercury was elected. He felt a pope should not have the name of a Roman god. Benedict is one of the most popular papal names, as shown by this list. These are names that have been used more than ten times.

John	23	Leo	13
Gregory	16	Innocent	13
Benedict	16	Pius	12
Clement	14		

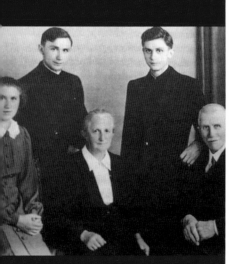

Joseph Ratzinger is seen in a photo dated July 8, 1951. Pictured from the left are Joseph's sister Maria, his brother Georg, his mother Maria, Joseph, and his father Joseph.

Bavaria is the most strongly Catholic region in Germany. It's said that growing up in this beautiful, mountainous area gives people such a sense of the wonder of God's creation that they cannot help but become strong Catholics. Apparently, that native love of God worked for Joseph and Georg, because both of them became priests. Joseph enrolled in the local minor seminary at the age of twelve, already sure that he had a vocation—a divine calling—to be a priest. That sense of certainty about his decisions would remain throughout his entire career in the church.

There would, however, be obstacles to overcome before he achieved this dream. The first obstacle was minor—the fact that he did not like being away from home at a boarding school. The next obstacle would dominate his life for several years—Hitler's rise to power. This would change his plans, just as it did for so many other Germans. His father's outspokenness against the Nazis cannot have made life easy for the Ratzinger children as Hitler's power grew. Joseph and Georg enrolled, as required, in the local Hitler Youth organization when Joseph was fourteen. He later remembered that he had managed not to attend the required meetings.

At age sixteen, he was drafted, along with other students from his school, into an anti-aircraft artillery unit by the German army. He would spend the next several years serving at various towns in the area. His duties involved mostly domestic defense—for example, guarding an aircraft engine plant. When his unit was finally released from service in 1944, he found himself facing the prospect of being drafted into the regular German army. After two months of building anti-tank defenses in Austria, he went through basic training but was lucky enough not to be sent to the front lines. Like many reluctant German soldiers, he deserted before the end of the war, once it seemed certain that the Allies were close to defeating Germany. As he headed back home, German soldiers captured him, but they let him go. With his arm in a sling from an injury, it was easy for them to excuse him as returning home because of his injury. He would later attribute his release to an angel watching over him.

When American troops arrived to occupy the area, they were not taking any chances on German resistance. Former soldiers like Joseph were rounded up and detained in prisoner-of-war camps as the area was stabilized. It would not be a long stay, and he was allowed to return home in June 1945. His brother, who had been a prisoner of war in Italy, also made it home safely. Finally, the two were able to resume their studies, this time at the major seminary in Freising. Their sister, Maria, worked to support the family so the brothers could attend school. On June 29, 1951, Joseph and his brother were ordained as priests together. The family celebrated the event by having a family photo taken. At twenty-four, Joseph Alois Ratzinger had achieved his first goal. He was a priest. It was, he would write, "the high point of my life."

PRIEST AND POPULAR TEACHER

As a person who believed he was "touched by Christ's mission" and "empowered to bring his nearness to men," Ratzinger gladly took on his new duties as an assistant pastor at a parish in Munich. His memoirs make it obvious that every part of his new life challenged and delighted him. He would be there only a year before being reassigned to the seminary in Freising to obtain a doctoral degree in theology. He wrote of his parents' joy at his graduation in July 1953. It seemed that church leaders were also pleased with his quick mind and talents at teaching. He was given a series of teaching assignments that would occupy him in the academic world for almost thirty years. Ratzinger taught at several universities over this time period. He was a popular teacher and much in demand, teaching to overflowing classes.

Ratzinger also served as a theological consultant to Cardinal Joseph Frings of Cologne during the Second Vatican Council. The young Ratzinger was already an influential presence, and contributed to one of the most famous speeches of the council, given by Cardinal Frings. During that time, he was known as a strong supporter of church reform, and he still considers himself to be so. However, when he returned to teaching, this time at the University of Tübingen, he witnessed events that forever changed his views on the course the church must take in modernizing.

In the late 1960s, there was a strong student protest movement on college campuses in Europe, especially in Germany and France. The students were pushing for more democratic participation in the political process and rejecting their governments' military activities. This movement had the support of many European Catholics. They saw political democracy as a reflection of Vatican II's emphasis on collegiality, with church authority spread out among the bishops.

Ratzinger, however, had a different reaction. He watched in horror as students at his school began to attack the church as part of their attacks on other elements of society. He soon left his post at Tübingen for a more conservative teaching setting at the University of Regensburg.

At this point in his life, Ratzinger came to a firm conclusion. The church must not allow dissidents the power to destroy traditional practices. In his writings, he shared his concern at how "agitated" the church was becoming. He warned against what he saw as "the impression that nothing stood fast in the church, that everything was up for revision." To many, it seemed that this was the end of his days as a reformer. He would say, however, that he still believed (then and now) in the reforms of Vatican II. Nevertheless, he had come to believe in the need to keep strict control over change. The church hierarchy should control the pace of change, maintain traditional beliefs, exercise tight control over dissidents, and keep experimentation and questioning within reasonable bounds. This view would become the basis for what many saw as a radically conservative outlook in the years to come.

PAPAL FRIEND

Moving up through the church hierarchy, Ratzinger was named archbishop of Munich and Freising in March 1977. Three months later, Pope Paul VI named him a cardinal. In 1978, Pope Paul VI died, and then his successor died in his sleep after only a month in office. The new conclave selected Karol Wojtyla as the new pope.

Ratzinger and Wojtyla had met in the conclave that elected Pope John Paul I in August 1978. However, both men knew of each other even before they met. They were both rising intellectuals in the church. Both shared a strong, reasoned faith and a love of knowledge for its own sake. Both felt the need to protect the church from runaway change. It was not surprising that Pope John Paul II would turn to Joseph Ratzinger in 1981 when he needed to appoint a new prefect to head the Congregation for the Doctrine of the Faith. This is the Vatican office responsible for safeguarding Catholic doctrine.

The post of prefect was a difficult position to hold. It required a man strong in his beliefs and willing to endure harsh criticism from both sides on any issue. In the modern Catholic Church, which represents such a wide variety of peoples, in widely varying economic, cultural, and

The Inquisition

The Congregation for the Doctrine of the Faith is the successor to the Office of the Inquisition. The church tribunal known as the Inquisition was formed in 1231 to combat a series of heresies, or false beliefs, that were seen as a threat to the church. This office began at a time when church and state functioned as one unit. Consequently, divisions caused by those who questioned any facet of church teaching were seen as potential threats to the stability of all of Europe. The Inquisition quickly became associated in the public mind with fear, torture, and death.

social situations, it would be impossible for everyone to be pleased by any pronouncement from the head of the congregation. Such was the situation for Cardinal Joseph Ratzinger. He made enemies with the decisions issued by the office. In doing so, he allowed Pope John Paul II to concentrate on making friends.

Although it was not an easy position, Cardinal Ratzinger fulfilled this role well. For Pope John Paul II, he was a staunch ally and, over the years, became a close friend. However, performing his job well presented a problem. It wasn't likely to get him elected as the next pope. He would not be seen as the charismatic and diplomatic leader that the next pope would have to be.

There was also a personal price to be paid for working in Rome. It would remove him from the country that he loved so well. His sister, Maria, came with him to Rome to become his secretary and house-keeper in his apartment near Vatican City. The two of them visited their brother and their homeland as often as possible, but Joseph missed his home. A friend of his, Munich banker Thaddaeus Kuehnel, remembered that loneliness and how he would "bring Bavaria to Rome" for Cardinal Ratzinger over the years. Kuehnel made several trips a year to Rome to deliver Bavarian sausages from Ratzinger's favorite restaurant, along with fruit nectar, candy, and Bavarian Christmas trees and Advent wreaths. This very human image of the cardinal is hard to reconcile with the harsh comments that would be made about him as he entered his papacy.

Many cats await their dinner near Trajan's Forum in Rome.

NINE

The Controversial New Pope

Anyone who has ever spent time in Rome knows that the city has a huge population of feral, or wild, cats. It sometimes seems that there are more cats than people. So the news that the new pope is a cat lover—or, as one headline put it, a "Lover of Cats, Cookies, and Conversation"—should have been only a cute little human-interest story about Benedict XVI. The accounts of his carefully caring for stray cats around his apartment near the Vatican, and of the cats following him around whenever he came out from Mass, would normally have resulted in humorous stories about the new "shepherd" of the Catholic Church ministering to a different kind of "flock." However, in the case of Benedict XVI, these stories had a much more serious purpose. They were needed to counter negative stories that used another animal image—that of a powerful, German-bred guard dog called a rottweiler—to refer to the new pope.

A SHOCKING CHOICE

Archbishop John Foley, serving as a commentator for the media, conversed with news anchor Brian Williams while the world waited to hear the new pope's name. Foley shared the newsman's surprise at how fast a decision had come. When asked whether a fast decision was good or bad, Foley replied that he was "delighted." Such a quick decision process meant that there was a great deal of agreement within the conclave on who should be elected pope.

Later leaks to the press showed that the archbishop's guesses were true. Apparently, the cardinal electors had little difficulty in making

The Vatican Museum

The Vatican houses one of the greatest libraries and art museums in the world. The Vatican Library has sixty-five thousand manuscripts and seven hundred thousand books in its collection. The museum, which includes the Sistine Chapel, was begun in 1503 and has 4.5 miles (7.2 kilometers) of galleries filled with paintings, sculptures, tapestries, and other works of art. Many of these artworks were made by some of the greatest classical and Renaissance artists, including Michelangelo, Raphael, and Leonardo da Vinci. It also has on display wonderful archaeological finds from Egypt, Greece, Rome, and pre-Roman times.

their decision. Some news accounts even claimed that Ratzinger had an overwhelming majority of votes—perhaps even as many as 107 of the 115 votes cast. It also appeared that, behind the doors of the Sistine Chapel, the other papabili never really posed any threat to Ratzinger's candidacy. The only other likely candidate had been Cardinal Carlo Maria Martini, the retired archbishop of Milan. Known as less conservative than most of the cardinals, the quiet, scholarly man was believed to have been ruled out for health reasons, even though he was the same age as Cardinal Ratzinger.

The selection of Ratzinger, and the fact that his only real competitor was equally old, indicated that the cardinal electors had decided to choose a caretaker rather than an activist, one of the three issues in determining a successor. They also chose to stay with a traditional Westerner. And third, by choosing

White smoke coming from a chimney on the Sistine Chapel's roof indicates a new pope has been elected.

The Pope's Real Church

S t. Peter's Basilica is not the official church of the pope. The pope also serves as bishop of the diocese of Rome, and the cathedral church of this diocese is the Basilica of St. John Lateran. It stands a few miles away from the Vatican. The Roman emperor Constantine gave the Lateran Palace to Pope Sylvester around A.D. 311, and the palace was converted into a basilica.

Ratzinger, they made a strong statement in favor of having someone with a conservative stance.

THE ONE-TIME PROGRESSIVE

Judging in advance how a pope will act during his papacy is not an easy task. Even the cardinal electors can be surprised by the decisions made by the person they elect as pope. This was apparent in the case of Pope John XXIII, and in 2005, the new pope's actions would prove to be difficult to predict as well. This was partly because Ratzinger had supported what appeared to be two radically different viewpoints during his long years of service to the church.

Cardinal Ratzinger was viewed as favoring reform at the time of Vatican II. Many say that when he was head of the Congregation for the Doctrine of the Faith two decades later, he was simply playing the conservative role that the position required. Others were not so generous. Theologian Hans Kung, for example, accused him of "selling his soul" for Vatican power.

Nevertheless, this new pope still sees himself as a reformer. He has repeatedly indicated that he feels he acts in the true spirit of Vatican II. He says he has been consistent in his theological positions. He believes that only those who willfully misinterpret the decrees of Vatican II find him to be too conservative.

Those who strongly oppose Ratzinger's views spoke angrily after his election. He was called "God's Rottweiler" and "Cardinal No." Another label was the Panzerkardinal, a reference to Germany's World War II panzer battle tanks. Unlike most new popes, who emerge relatively unknown, this pope was known for his unpopular stands. He also had many published works, which gave his detractors ample ammunition for

Cardinal Ratzinger (center) and Venezuelan archbishop Rosalio Jose Castillo Lara (right) observe Pope John Paul II in January 1983. The pope was signing a law that, among other things, made it more difficult to have a marriage annulled.

attacking him. However, his unpopular views were often those also held by Pope John Paul II. One of the more amusing media comments from the early days of the new papacy was that selecting Cardinal Ratzinger to succeed John Paul II was the closest the Catholic Church had ever come to allowing cloning. Humorous as it was, the comment also reflected the reality that these men held strongly similar theological views.

THE ENFORCER

Cardinal Ratzinger headed the Congregation for the Doctrine of the Faith for more than twenty years (1981–2005). Many have commented that, during that time, he played the role of zealous enforcer for Pope John Paul II. Others, however, argue that Ratzinger's views were very much his own. They point to Ratzinger's own words in the homily he

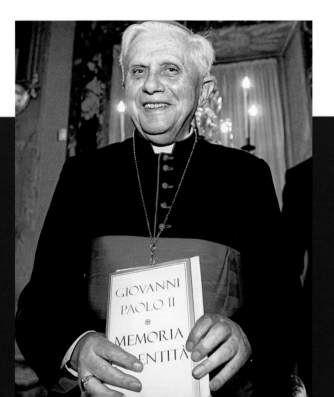

Cardinal Joseph Ratzinger holds a copy of a book written by Pope John Paul II. The cardinal served as the head of the Vatican Congregation for the Doctrine of the Faith.

preached at the opening of the conclave that elected him pope. He took strong stands and spoke his mind very clearly—so clearly, in fact, that many commentators felt he had just ruined any chance he had of being elected pope. Cardinal Ratzinger preached against what he called "a dictatorship of relativism." He shared with his fellow cardinals his fear of witnessing a world and a faith that had lost all certainty.

The views he expressed in his homily were a good summary of what he had been saying for years. They also reflect the views of many Catholics around the world. There has been much dissension and division among Catholics as a result of Vatican II, sometimes resulting in whole groups actually breaking away from the church. This situation was of great concern to the late pope. Thus, he chose a strong and articulate enforcer to make sure that the church's message remained a unified one.

As part of his duties, Cardinal Ratzinger had been responsible for making sure that theologians were adhering to the church's approved teachings. This proved to be a controversial role because of differing views of Catholic doctrine. One view is that Catholic theology is unchanging over time. Another view, endorsed by Vatican II, is that divine revelation, and thus theology, is an ongoing process throughout human history. Ratzinger's insistence on unchanging doctrine put him in conflict with many well-known Catholic educators around the world. His former associate, Hans Kung, was denied the right to teach theology because he refused to conform to church teachings. In 1986, Ratzinger informed U.S. theologian Charles Curran that he was "not suitable nor eligible to teach Catholic theology," even though Curran's teaching met the criteria set by U.S. bishops for those teaching at Catholic universities.

Critics of the new pope feel that his controversial positions go beyond issues within the church. These critics view his outlook on ecumenism with alarm. He was reported to have characterized Buddhism as a religion for the self-indulgent. He told a French reporter that Turkey should not be allowed to join the European Union because of its strong Muslim population. One of his books also criticized multiculturalism in Europe. Such feelings shatter the hopes of a more universally oriented church, especially for those who feel the church should be in the forefront of uniting people of different faiths around the world. As cardinal, Ratzinger published a book in which he said, "We might have to part with the notion of a popular church." This view—often called Ratzinger's Mustard Seed, from a biblical quotation in the book—calls for a smaller, doctrinally pure church made up of those willing "to bear the yoke of Christ."

Ratzinger has also made enemies by calling to task those who supported liberation theology and religious pluralism (the view that all religions are equally valid and true). He also earned the anger of many for refusing to allow internal dissent on such church issues as married priests or the ordination of women. Critics feel he interfered in the outreach of the Catholic Church to minister to gays and lesbians because of his belief that homosexuality was a "moral evil," a position that angered many in the United States. He even became involved in a controversy that touched on the 2004 presidential election when he suggested that voting for a politician who supports such "grave sins" as abortion might also be a grave sin. He condemned all such examples of "radical individualism" in the church.

Some Catholics feel that the rigid positions of the Congregation for the Doctrine of the Faith under Cardinal Ratzinger opened the church to criticism and increased division over issues that were unworthy of the attention they received. Examples include official attacks made by the church on two works of popular literature, *The Da Vinci Code* (because it was "a clear attempt to discredit the Church") and the Harry Potter series (for the black magic in the stories). Ratzinger condemned modern music for its anti-religious tone as far back as 1986. Thus, taking a stand against popular culture is not unusual for him. Intervening so strongly in what many see as minor issues tends to reinforce the public impression of the pope as extremely zealous in his beliefs and unwilling (or unable) to show respect for differing viewpoints, even in relatively minor matters.

THE BELIEVER

Clearly, Pope Benedict XVI arouses strong feelings among those who disagree with him. However, he engenders equally strong support among those who see in him the "rock" that Jesus envisioned Saint Peter and his succes-

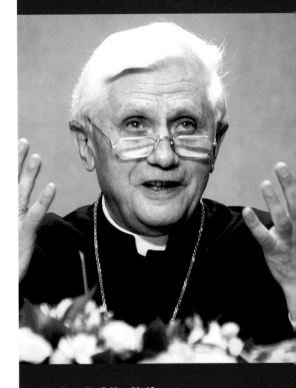

As head of the Vatican Congregation for the Doctrine of the Faith Cardinal Ratzinger holds a news conference in June 2000 to disclose the Vatican's stand on the meaning behind the "Third Secret of Fatima." The Vatican believes Sister Lucia de Jesus dos Santos had a series of visions foretelling the 1981 assassination attempt against Pope John Paul II.

sors to be. Ratzinger, as a cardinal, had the unusual distinction of having a fan club. A group of supporters organized the Ratzinger Fan Club to answer what they felt was unfair criticism of his positions. This group, whose members studied Ratzinger's writings, introduced their Web site with the statement that they "have come to admire him both as brilliant Catholic theologian but also as a man whose faith, honesty, integrity, and unswerving devotion to the Truth is readily apparent." They were delighted when the cardinal electors showed by their vote that they found Cardinal Ratzinger a worthy successor to Pope John Paul II.

On his first visit to the balcony where he was presented to the world, Pope Benedict XVI was the picture of goodwill. Although shy, he smiled and waved and seemed quite surprised at the intensity of the cheering crowds. He responded with humor and with promises to keep the personnel and the policies of his predecessor.

In spite of previous comments about other religions, he pledged to "continue building bridges of friendship" with other faiths. His inaugural Mass was attended by Muslim, Buddhist, Eastern Orthodox, and Jewish leaders, as well as leaders of various Protestant denominations. He promised the world that he, as pope, was not there to "pursue my own ideas." He promised to be a listener to others' views.

In terms of church policies, he reappointed church officials originally selected by Pope John Paul II and repeatedly voiced his intention to follow the decisions his predecessor had made. He also made clear that he planned to use modern technology, and his e-mail address appeared within a few days of his election. He also recognized and thanked the world media for their coverage of Pope John Paul II's death and funeral and his own election as pope, and he promised a "dialogue" with the media.

As an important first step in diffusing his severe image, he brought humor into his discussions. Apologizing to a group of Germans because he was late for a meeting, he noted their German punctuality, but then added that he had become an Italian during his time in Italy. He repeatedly addressed the world humbly, as "a servant of God."

Ultimately, as with any new pope, it will take time to see the direction that this new papacy will follow. Popes, like presidents, are changed by the responsibilities of their office. Their tenures are often judged more kindly by history than by the media, with their instant analysis of decisions and simplistic explanations of the issues. It will be interesting to see how Pope Benedict XVI responds to the issues facing the Catholic Church in the twenty-first century—issues that have become his responsibility.

When the new pope was installed on Sunday, April 24, 2005, many representatives from various Orthodox churches were in attendance. Many people also traveled from Germany for the event.

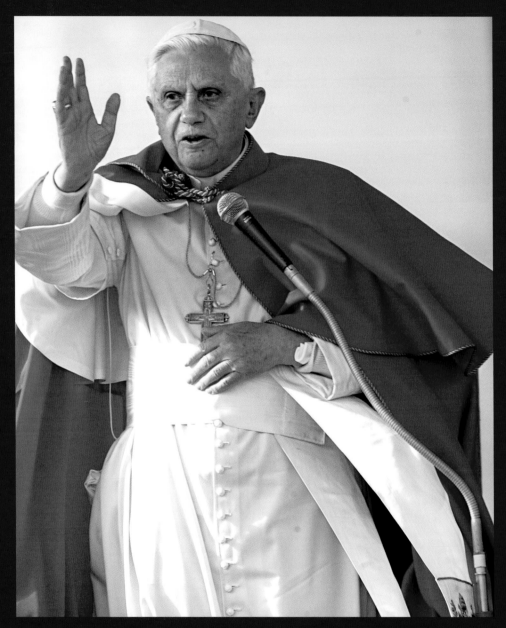

Giving blessings is an important part of the pope's responsibility. People travel from all over the world to see him in St. Peter's Square.

TEN

Benedict XVI and the Future of the Catholic Church

Pope Benedict XVI will face many major issues in his papacy, whether he serves for a long or short time. It is no easy task for any pope to reconcile the needs of more than one billion Catholics living in totally diverse societies with divergent views. Pope Benedict must deal with the ongoing issues of social and economic justice around the world, the push for ecumenism among religious groups, and the subject of collegiality within the church. The decrease in the numbers of priests will remain a major problem as well.

Many scholars of religion see a trend in the West toward increasing religious fervor. At the same time, other observers point to an increasing secularism—a focus on worldly concerns rather than on spiritual values. They see this trend as one of Pope Benedict's greatest challenges. The pope must also deal with beliefs in the West regarding sexual mores—for example, on the issues of birth control and abortion—and other contentious topics such as euthanasia (helping a terminally ill person die) and the use of extraordinary means to prolong life. All these topics were of continuing concern to the last pope. They would have been of concern to whomever had been elected after him.

MATERIALISM AND THE CLERGY ISSUE

Pope John Paul II was bitterly disappointed by what happened in Poland once the Polish people were free of their communist regime. There, where the faith of the people had carried them through communism and helped them maintain their unity, that faith lost its strength in the face of capitalism. As with other European and American Catholics, growing prosperity brought increased use of birth control and increased numbers of divorces. As one commentator wrote, they "flocked to purchase CDs and BMWs and cell phones."

One of the major issues that Pope Benedict XVI must deal with is the increased materialism that has followed in every country where the standard of living has been raised. As people focus on material things, they can easily turn away from their faith. As a cardinal, Ratzinger had expressed his fear that Europe, by "disdaining God completely," had brought the world "to the edge of the abyss." Whether one agrees with his analysis or not, there is no doubt that the church hierarchy needs to relate to Catholics in these countries. Not only does the church need to strengthen their faith, but it also needs their financial support, which allows the church to function. Their funds finance Catholic ministries in the Third World, where the number of Catholics grew during John Paul II's papacy.

The pope's task will become even more difficult in the coming years as the shortage of priests becomes critical. Especially among American Catholics, who increasingly are involved in the day-to-day running of their parishes, many see obvious answers to the declining number of priests—allowing priests to marry and ordaining women. Both issues are hot buttons for the Vatican Curia, the church's administrative and governing body. The Curia not only has forbidden Catholics to consider these options, but has also tried to curb discussion of them. This has been especially hard for members of democracies that thrive on free speech. With about one in six parishes in the United States without a priest, and with the aging of the existing clergy, this is an issue that will only become more pressing in the years ahead.

The United States, in particular, has also suffered a crisis from the sexual abuse of young people by priests. This crisis has been seen as a bit-

Father Gregory Beyer says Mass at a shopping mall. Catholic centers provide spiritual outreach and support in an environment where one would not expect to find it.

ter betrayal of youth by the church hierarchy. More than seven hundred priests have been removed from their posts for sexual abuse, and the church has paid out more than $1 billion to victims. Many Catholics felt that the Vatican did not take the issue seriously and did not give support when it was most needed. Decisions made after the death of John Paul II only rubbed salt into the wound, as American Catholics saw Cardinal Bernard Law featured as one of the celebrants of the nine special Masses offered for the late pope. Catholic wrath over the sexual abuse issue had focused on Cardinal Law for protecting priests who were known pedophiles (child molesters). Seeing Law chosen for this public role was not well received in many quarters.

Pope Benedict XVI will have to devise solutions of some kind to these issues in the Western church. With aging clergy, declining numbers of priests, and an angry congregation in the United States, even a short papacy (which the pope himself has predicted) will require difficult decisions be made for Western Catholicism. On his first foreign trip as pope—to Germany, a Western country—Pope Benedict's major sermon

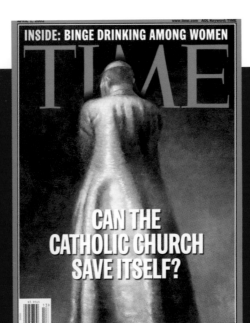

INSIDE: BINGE DRINKING AMONG WOMEN

TIME

CAN THE CATHOLIC CHURCH SAVE ITSELF?

This cover from the April 1, 2002, issue of *Time* magazine illustrates the scandal which has rocked the Catholic Church. Some people have left the church because of the sexual abuse scandal.

was on the subject of "the strange forgetfulness of God" that he saw in the West today. Yet, many Western Catholics will no longer be content to "Pay, Pray, and Obey," as an old saying goes.

"LIFE" ISSUES

Pope Benedict XVI's papacy will also face what are called the life issues. Many see the declining church attendance in the West as the result of Pope Paul VI's encyclical *Humanae Vitae* ("Of Human Life"), which banned the use of contraception. For most Western Catholics, there is a widening gap between what the church teaches and what Catholics choose to follow. Nowhere is this more apparent than in the issue of birth control. Surveys indicate that the overwhelming majority of Western Catholics simply ignore church rulings forbidding the use of contraceptives.

A broader "life" issue is the epidemic of AIDS (acquired immuno-deficiency syndrome) in Africa. About 64 percent of the world's AIDS patients live in southern Africa. The disease can be spread in a number of ways, including sexual activity. Despite evidence that using condoms might halt the spread of AIDS, and despite pleas from health organizations around the world, the Vatican has adamantly refused to allow Catholics to use condoms. Vatican leaders simply answer that abstinence from sexual activity is the only available option, whether for birth control or for preventing the spread of sexually transmitted diseases. As the number of AIDS victims grows, it becomes increasingly obvious that abstinence as a policy is not going to solve the life-and-death problem facing African Catholics today. At the same time, many Catholics see this as a watershed issue—an

Members of a church in Managua, Nicaragua, worship during Mass. Many people see the need for the church to focus on the problems of Third World Countries such as poverty, AIDS, and lack of education.

issue on which the church must continue to take a strong moral stand.

A word that often appears in discussions of the new pope is "intransigent." That means firmly refusing to consider changing a decision or attitude. Early in his papacy, Pope Benedict preached a sermon praising his predecessor who, "faced with erroneous interpretations of freedom, underlined in an unequivocal way, the inviolability of human beings, the inviolability of human life from conception to natural death."

In that sermon, the pope clearly summarized a serious division in the church. There are differing interpretations of freedom among Catholics today. Many feel that the AIDS crisis shows a critical need for a new freedom of thought. It calls for flexible and creative thinking on the part of the church and the entire human race. Because of this, Pope Benedict XVI will face increasing world pressure to temper the church's teachings about contraception with understanding for AIDS victims. At the same time, many other Catholics feel that a change in church policy on this issue would mean abandoning a critical tenet of their belief. Those Catholics need Pope Benedict XVI to be intransigent. Finding the correct path for the church is an extremely challenging task for the pope.

THE THIRD WORLD AND ITS DIFFERING NEEDS

More than 40 percent of the world's Catholics live in Latin America. Another 13 percent live in Africa. More than 10 percent of Catholics live in Asia, and that number is growing rapidly. In fact, North America and Europe now account for less than one-third of the worldwide Catholic population. The overwhelming majority of the world's Catholics live in underdeveloped countries and face issues of day-to-day survival. They look to the church to support them in their needs.

The economic inequality among the regions of the world is a critical issue facing Pope Benedict XVI as he tries to meet the needs of all Catholics. In Latin America, many Catholics have become disillusioned by the lack of church support for a more evenhanded distribution of the world's resources. Many Protestant groups have been making inroads among Catholic populations in Latin America, promising the people a more vibrant and activist religion.

With Catholics widespread around the globe, the church is in the best position of any single entity to address the economic imbalances in the world today. The new pope faces a challenge here—the challenge of bringing the Western one-third of his followers to understand their responsibility to help meet the needs of the other two-thirds of their brethren. Pope Benedict XVI also faces another challenge—to maintain the church's growth in Asia and Africa while preserving its numbers in Latin America.

Many Catholics in the Third World were angered by the election of yet another Western pope. For them, this showed that the church does not truly care about the needs of the majority of its members. This is an issue that truly demands flexibility and creative thinking. Pope Benedict XVI will need to assure these people that he is their pope, too.

ECUMENISM

Pope John Paul II was by far the most ecumenically oriented pope of modern times. An unprecedented number of leaders from other churches attended his funeral. This was a direct result of his reaching out to other religions and his efforts to bring religious leaders together. That effort to open lines of communication and understanding among religions is good not only for the religions themselves but also for the human race.

Religious conflict, especially between the Muslim and Christian worlds, is worse now than at any time since the Crusades (the eleventh through sixteenth centuries). The Christian military campaigns during

Pope Benedict XVI traveled to Cologne, Germany, for the twentieth World Youth Day. He said farewell to the participants in French, English, Spanish, Italian, Polish, Portuguese, Tagalog, Swahili, and German.

the Crusades were organized mainly to recapture the Holy Land from Muslim occupation. Today, the Muslim-Christian divide is a vital issue throughout the West, as immigration brings Muslim minorities into contact with traditionally Christian societies. Today, unlike at the time of the Crusades, the potential for world carnage exists if these two groups cannot either settle their differences or resolve to live in peace with each other.

As cardinal, Joseph Ratzinger published a paper titled *Dominus Jesus* ("Lord Jesus"). It took a strong position that there was only one true church and that was the Roman Catholic Church. Such a view does not seem to leave room for compromise in dealing with other religions. As pope, however, Benedict XVI has different responsibilities than he had as head of the Congregation for the Doctrine of the Faith. His challenge will be to make the Vatican a force for peace and unity by continuing on the ecumenical journey begun by John Paul II. The new pope has shown that he intends to do this.

Early in his papacy, Pope Benedict made efforts to engage in dialogue with Eastern Orthodox, Jewish, and Muslim leaders. These gestures were seen as a sign of his intentions to continue John Paul's legacy of friendly relations with other religions. On his first trip out of Italy— to Cologne, Germany, for World Youth Day in August 2005—he visited a synagogue and spoke out against what he called "new signs of anti-Semitism" in the world. The next day, he met with Muslim leaders, expressing hope that they could work together in peace. He also appealed to them to help combat the spread of terrorism, which was "sowing death and destruction." Only time will reveal whether Benedict XVI will leave as striking a legacy as his predecessor in this critical area.

TWO POPES, ONE PAPACY

The Catholic Church has always been known for its constancy—for continuing to be faithful to its ideals, beliefs, and decisions. This was apparent with the election of Benedict XVI. He had represented Pope John Paul II toward the end of his life and had played a major role in church decision making for most of John Paul's papacy. In many ways, the early months of Pope Benedict XVI's reign seemed little more than a continuation of things as they had been under his predecessor.

Personnel remained essentially the same. Policy remained the same, as did statements about the need to hold firmly to traditional Catholic beliefs. Outreach to other faiths continued along the path that John Paul II had laid out. In terms of his moral stands, experts felt that Benedict XVI had, as expected, continued to defend his strong views on moral and life issues, the views he shared with his predecessor.

In fact, as the first months of his papacy came to an end, many concluded that 2005 might become known as the year of two popes, but only one papacy. What legacy Pope Benedict XVI will leave will depend in part on whether he moves away from a strict continuation of John Paul II's policies and decisions and steers the church on a different course.

Pope Benedict XVI became pope in contentious times, and he holds a position that is increasingly difficult. It requires a person of strong faith and great willingness to listen to others with understanding and sympathy for their needs. It also requires a person with the courage to take stands that will always be unpopular with at least some portion of the church's vast membership. Perhaps it is good that the cardinal electors chose someone who is fond of saying that "Truth is not determined by a majority vote."

Timeline

**THE LIVES OF
POPE JOHN PAUL II
AND POPE BENEDICT XVI** WORLD EVENTS

1920 Karol Jozef Wojtyla is born in Wadowice, Poland, on May 18.

1927 Joseph Alois Ratzinger is born in Marktl am Inn in Bavaria, Germany, on April 16.

1929 Wojtyla's mother dies.

1933 The Nazi Party under Adolf Hitler takes power in Germany.

1938 Wojtyla and his father move to Krakow, Poland, where Karol enrolls in Jagiellonian University.

1939 German Nazis close down Jagiellonian University. Ratzinger begins studying for the priesthood.

Hitler's Nazi troops invade Poland on September 1; World War II begins.

1941 Wojtyla's father dies.

1942 Wojtyla begins secretly studying for the priesthood in Krakow.

1943 Ratzinger is drafted into the German army.

1944 Hitler destroys Warsaw, Poland's capital city.

1945 The Soviet Union occupies Poland. World War II ends.

1946 Wojtyla is ordained a priest on November 1.

1948 Wojtyla earns a doctorate at the Angelicum in Rome, Italy. He begins his ministry as assistant pastor at a parish in Niegowic, Poland.

1951 Wojtyla begins his studies for a doctorate in philosophy at Jagiellonian University. Ratzinger and his brother, Georg, are ordained as priests in Freising, Germany, on June 29.

1953 Ratzinger earns a doctorate in theology at the University of Munich.

1958 Wojtyla is made auxiliary bishop of Krakow on July 4, becoming Poland's youngest bishop. Pope Pius XXII dies on October 9, and Cardinal Angelo Roncalli succeeds him as Pope John XXIII.

1960 Wojtyla publishes his first nonfiction book, *Love and Responsibility*.

1962–1965 Pope John XXIII convenes the Second Vatican Council (Vatican II). During the council, Ratzinger serves as consultant to Cardinal Joseph Frings.

1963 Pope John XXIII dies on June 3; Pope Paul VI succeeds him. Wojtyla is appointed archbishop of Krakow on December 30.

1966 Ratzinger begins teaching at the University of Tübingen.

1967 Pope Paul VI consecrates Wojtyla as a cardinal on June 26.

1977 Ratzinger becomes archbishop of Munich and Freising on March 25. He becomes a cardinal on June 27.

1978 Pope Paul VI dies on August 6. Cardinal Albino Luciani of Venice is elected pope on August 26, taking the name Pope John Paul I. He dies on September 28. Cardinal Wojtyla is elected pope on October 16, choosing the name Pope John Paul II.

1979 Pope John Paul II visits Poland, his homeland. In the United States, he becomes the first pope ever to visit the White House.

1981 Pope John Paul II is shot and seriously wounded by Turkish gunman Mehmet Ali Agca on May 13. John Paul II appoints Cardinal Ratzinger as prefect of the Congregation for the Doctrine of the Faith on November 25.

1989 Poland's Solidarity movement achieves free elections and succeeds in ousting the country's Soviet-led communist government.

1991 The Soviet Union breaks apart as its communist regime collapses.

1992 Pope John Paul II has a tumor removed from his large intestine.

1995 In his encyclical *Ut Unum Sint* ("That They May Be One"), Pope John Paul II calls for greater unity among the world's religions.

1998 Pope John Paul II makes a plea for religion and science to work together in his encyclical *Fides et Ratio* ("Faith and Reason").

2001 On a visit to Syria, Pope John Paul II becomes the first pope ever to visit a Muslim mosque.

2002 Cardinal Ratzinger is elected dean of the College of Cardinals.

2005 Pope John Paul II dies in his apartment in Vatican City on April 2. Cardinal Ratzinger is elected pope on April 19 and takes the name Pope Benedict XVI. On his first trip as pope, he visits Cologne, Germany, for World Youth Day.

To Find Out More

BOOKS

Behnke, Alison M. *Pope John Paul II*. Minneapolis: Lerner, 2006.

Burns, Peggy. *Pope John Paul II: Pope for the People*. Austin, TX: Raintree Steck-Vaughn, 2001.

Glossop, Jennifer. *The Kids Book of World Religions*. Tonawanda, NY: Kids Can Press, 2003.

Klein, Virginia D., and Richard A. Klein. *Dear Papa: Children Celebrate Pope John Paul II with Letters of Love and Affection*. Liguori, MO: Liguori/Triumph, 2003.

Palmer, Martin. *Religions of the World*. New York: Checkmark Books, 2005.

Sullivan, Maureen. *101 Questions and Answers on Vatican II*. Mahwah, NJ: Paulist Press, 2003.

Vereb, Jerome M., ed. *Every Child a Light: The Pope's Message to Young People / John Paul II*. Honesdale, PA: Boyds Mills Press, 2002.

ORGANIZATIONS AND ONLINE SITES

The Pope's E-mail Address
benedictxvi@vatican.va

People can e-mail Pope Benedict XVI at his address.

Ratzinger Fan Club
www.popebenedictxvifanclub.com

This fan club existed (as www.ratzingerfanclub.com) even before Cardinal Ratzinger became Pope Benedict XVI. It lists up-to-date information about his activities and writings and even sells T-shirts and sweatshirts.

Vatican Web Site (English)
www.vatican.va/phome_en.htm

On this Web site, if you click on "Holy Father" and then on "Benedict XVI," you can read an official biography of the pope and all of his latest speeches and sermons. You can also click on John Paul II for his biography, encyclicals, and other writings.

A Note on Sources

There are several excellent biographies of Pope John Paul II available. The most authoritative is the one by George Weigel, *Witness to Hope: The Biography of Pope John Paul II* (New York: HarperCollins, 1999). Three other thorough accounts, which I both enjoyed and found useful, are Carl Bernstein and Marco Politi's *His Holiness: John Paul II and the Hidden History of Our Time* (New York: Doubleday, 1996), Jonathan Kwitny's *Man of the Century: The Life and Times of Pope John Paul II* (New York: Henry Holt and Company, 1997), and Tad Szulc's *Pope John Paul II: The Biography* (New York: Scribner, 1995).

For information about how popes are elected, I turned to one of my favorite books, *Saints & Sinners*, written by Eamon Duffy (New Haven, CT: Yale University Press, 1997). I supplemented that information with two other sources, Michael J. Walsh's *An Illustrated History of the Popes: Saint Peter to John Paul II* (New York: St. Martin's Press, 1980) and Andrew M. Greeley's *The Making of the Popes 1978* (Kansas City, MO): Andrews and McMeer, 1979).

During the conclave and immediately after the election of Benedict XVI, I was busy reading about ten newspapers and news sites online, from the *New York Times* and *Washington Post* to CNN and Fox News—and supplemented by BBC Online and Deutsche Welle for the European perspective. Because this was a Catholic Church issue, I was also interested in what Catholic publications, such as the *National Catholic Reporter* and *America*, were writing about both the conclave and the new pope. It was exciting to be reading about a current news story in such depth, something that I probably never would have done to this extent.

Pope Benedict XVI is a prolific writer, and one of his books in particular, *Milestones, 1927–1977* (Fort Collins, CO: Ignatius Press, 1998), gave a wonderful account of his early life. In addition, several of his other books introduce the reader to his beliefs about the church, especially *The Ratzinger Report* (San Francisco: Ignatius Press, 1985) and *Salt of the Earth: The Church at the End of the Millennium* (San Francisco: Ignatius Press, 1997). There is a critical biography of the new pope entitled *Pope Benedict XVI*, written by John L. Allen Jr. (New York: Continuum, 2000), which provided much information. Stephen Mansfield's *Pope Benedict XVI: His Life and Mission* (New York: Penguin, 2005) also provided a few anecdotes about his life.

—*Susan Provost Beller*

Index

About the Author

Susan Provost Beller is the author of fifteen books about history written for middle school and junior high students. Several of her titles are about the Revolutionary War and the Civil War. She considers herself "a teller of stories," specifically the real stories of history. A former school librarian, she also teaches teachers how to bring the history of Vermont into their classrooms through summer courses she teaches for the University of Vermont.

A resident of Charlotte, Vermont, when not writing and researching, she can be found traveling to historic sites with her husband or enjoying visits to her three grown children and her four grandchildren.

THE JUDAS COIN

THE JUDAS COIN

Written and illustrated by
WALTER SIMONSON

Colorist
LOVERN KINDZIERSKI

Letterer
JOHN WORKMAN

Cover by
WALTER SIMONSON

Colored by
LOVERN KINDZIERSKI

Associate Editor
CHRIS CONROY

Editor
JOEY CAVALIERI

Batman Created by **BOB KANE**

I would like to thank Mark Chiarello for fanning the spark that became **The Judas Coin**, Dan DiDio for encouraging me to create a graphic novel out of that spark, Joey Cavalieri and Chris Conroy for their commitment and editorial savvy over the long haul, and Terri Cunningham for her unwavering support.

I also want to thank John Workman and Lovern Kindzierski for making everything better, and Bryant Arms, Steve Hoveke, Dan King, and Thomas Kintner for their various contributions to the cause.

I would like to dedicate this modest volume to my best girl, Weezie, *sine qua non*, and to my father, with love. He didn't get to see it finished, but he was interested in it from Day 1. It's done, Pop.

JOEY CAVALIERI EDITOR
ROBBIN BROSTERMAN DESIGN DIRECTOR – BOOKS
LOUIS PRANDI PUBLICATION DESIGN

BOB HARRAS VP-EDITOR-IN-CHIEF

DIANE NELSON PRESIDENT
DAN DIDIO AND JIM LEE CO-PUBLISHERS
GEOFF JOHNS CHIEF CREATIVE OFFICER
JOHN ROOD EXECUTIVE VP – SALES, MARKETING AND BUSINESS DEVELOPMENT
AMY GENKINS SENIOR VP – BUSINESS AND LEGAL AFFAIRS
NAIRI GARDINER SENIOR VP – FINANCE
JEFF BOISON VP – PUBLISHING OPERATIONS
MARK CHIARELLO VP – ART DIRECTION AND DESIGN
JOHN CUNNINGHAM VP – MARKETING
TERRI CUNNINGHAM VP – TALENT RELATIONS AND SERVICES
ALISON GILL SENIOR VP – MANUFACTURING AND OPERATIONS
HANK KANALZ SENIOR VP – DIGITAL
JAY KOGAN VP – BUSINESS AND LEGAL AFFAIRS, PUBLISHING
JACK MAHAN VP – BUSINESS AFFAIRS, TALENT
NICK NAPOLITANO VP – MANUFACTURING ADMINISTRATION
SUE POHJA VP – BOOK SALES
COURTNEY SIMMONS SENIOR VP – PUBLICITY
BOB WAYNE SENIOR VP – SALES

LIBRARY OF CONGRESS CATALOGING-IN-PUBLICATION DATA

SIMONSON, WALTER.
THE JUDAS COIN / WALTER SIMONSON.
  P. CM.
ISBN 978-1-4012-1541-5
1. GRAPHIC NOVELS. I. TITLE.
PN6727.S523J83 2012
741.5'973--DC23
                2012018908

There was once a man who betrayed a friend for thirty pieces of silver.

He betrayed him with a kiss.

The friend was crucified.

INRI

...FOR THE SILVER COINS WERE NOW DEEMED TO BE BLOOD MONEY.

HE DIED A SUICIDE.

THE JUDAS COIN

HIS LEGACY ENDURES.

73 AD
THE GOLDEN GLADIATOR

69 AD was the Year of the Four Emperors. At the end of the twelve months, three were dead and the fourth ruled the Roman Empire. A soldier who had risen through the ranks to command armies, Titus Flavius Vespasianus fought in Britain and subdued a rebellion in Judea. He entered the Eternal City in 70 AD as the undisputed master of the Western world. But the laurel wreath rests uneasily upon the head of any who dare to wear it.

BLOODPEACE

VESPASIAN HAS BEEN EMPEROR OF ROME FOR FIVE YEARS.

ROMAN ROADS LEAD EVERY-WHERE...

...EVEN TO THE RIVER RHINE IN THE FORESTS OF GERMANIA...

...THE EDGE OF THE EMPIRE.

THE BREEZE IS CHILLY...

...A HARBINGER OF THE WINTER THAT IS WAITING IN THE WINGS.

FINALLY!

LANDLORD, **BEER!** AND WHATEVER SWILL PASSES FOR FOOD IN THIS GODFORSAKEN WILDERNESS.

A GENTLER TONGUE MIGHT BE WISE. WE **ARE** BEYOND THE RHINE HERE. AND A LONG WAY FROM ROME.

AS IF I DIDN'T KNOW IT. I HAVEN'T SLEPT SO ROUGH IN YEARS. MY OLD SOLDIER'S BONES ACHE WITH COLD.

THROW ANOTHER LOG ON THE FIRE. YOU WANT US TO FREEZE TO DEATH?

LEGIONARIES ARE AS RARE AS HEN'S TEETH HEREABOUTS.

WILL YOU JOIN ME, TRAVELERS, AND SHARE MY MEAGER SUPPER?

WITH PLEASURE, STRANGER. COME, MARCUS.

A GOOD ROMAN NAME, SOLDIER. AND YOU...?

I HAVE NO NAME. I AM MERELY CAESAR'S MESSENGER, SEEKING A LOCAL NAMED TRAHERN.

YOU HAVE FOUND HIM, MY NAMELESS FRIEND. SO SPEAK TO ME OF SILVER. HAVE YOU BROUGHT IT?

MORE THAN YOU'VE EVER SEEN. CAREFULLY GUARDED AGAINST **TREACHERY** FOR THE PRESENT. HERE IS AN **EARNEST** OF OUR GOOD INTENTIONS.

YOUR FULL REWARD COMES **AFTER** OUR MISSION IS ACCOMPLISHED.

A TYRIAN SHEKEL.

AND GENUINE.

YOU WEAR YOUR ARROGANCE TOO OPENLY, ROMAN, BUT THE GODS FAVOR YOU...FOR NOW. THE LEADER OF THE REBELLION WILL BE HERE, IN THIS VERY INN TONIGHT.

ONE QUICK THRUST OF A SHORT SWORD COULD END THE UPRISING.

I'LL SEE YOU IN THE MORNING, GENTLEMEN. TRY NOT TO DIE BEFORE YOU DELIVER THE REST OF MY SILVER.

YOU THINK HE'S TELLING THE TRUTH?

JUPITER'S ASS, THIS BEER IS AWFUL.

HE'S A TRAITOR. IT'S JUST A QUESTION OF WHO HE'S BETRAYING.

THAT WOULD BE US.

DON'T HURT THEM. NOT YET.

IF MY HALF-BROTHER WAS TELLING THE TRUTH, WE'VE CAUGHT A PRIZE THIS NIGHT.

TRAHERN SAID CAESAR **HIMSELF** WAS COMING TO SANCTION THE PACT.

LET US SEE WHO HAS BETRAYED WHOM.

THIS ISN'T CAESAR! I DON'T--

MARCUS!

ARDRA!!!

MARCUS! I...CAN'T BELIEVE...

...YOUR HAIR! IT'S GRAY.

LIKE VENUS, ARDRA, YOU HAVE REMAINED AGELESS. I AM MERELY MORTAL AND MUST BOW BEFORE THE TYRANNY OF TIME.

BUT--

GUUKK!

I BELIEVE THAT **I** AM TITUS FLAVIUS CAESAR VESPASIAN. MARCUS AND I THOUGHT IT AS WELL TO SWITCH ROLES FOR THE NIGHT.

AND YOU WOULD BE THE MYSTERIOUS REBEL LEADER WHO'S BEEN CAUSING MY TROOPS IN LOWER GERMANIA SO MUCH TROUBLE?

I DID TELL YOU, MARCUS, THAT TRAHERN WOULD BETRAY SOMEBODY.

INDEED, CAESAR.

BUT I CONFESS I AM CONFOUNDED. YOU **KNOW** THIS SPITFIRE?

ONCE LONG AGO, IN ROME.

HER FATHER WAS INGULIUS.

THE WARRIOR WHO LED THE BATAVIANS AND NEARLY DEFEATED NERO'S LEGIONS.?

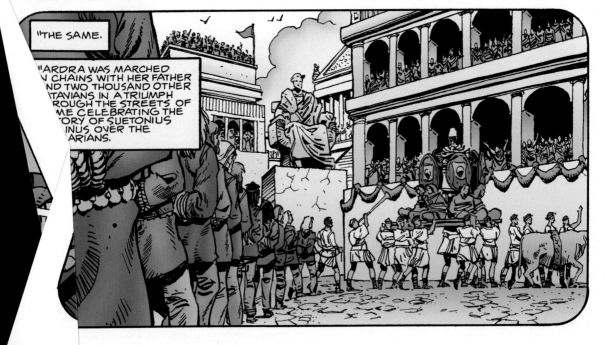

"THE SAME.

"ARDRA WAS MARCHED [IN] CHAINS WITH HER FATHER [A]ND TWO THOUSAND OTHER [BA]TAVIANS IN A TRIUMPH [TH]ROUGH THE STREETS OF [RO]ME CELEBRATING THE [VIC]TORY OF SUETONIUS [PAUL]INUS OVER THE [BARB]ARIANS.

"INGULIUS WAS EXECUTED BY THE EMPEROR.

"ARDRA'S RIGHT HAND WAS CUT OFF, AND SHE WAS THROWN TO THE LIONS WITH THE OTHER REBELS IN THE CELEBRATORY GAMES.

"THEY WERE TO HAVE BEEN MY LAST.

"WHEN EVERYONE ELSE WAS DEAD, THE FINAL LION CAME FOR HER. SHE STOOD THERE ALONE AND DEFIANT, WOUNDED...

"...AWAITING HER DEATH WITH AS MUCH COURAGE AS ANY ROMAN.

"I COULD NOT LET HER DIE.

"WE TWO ALONE SURVIVED.

"NERO WAS AMUSED BY THE SPECTACLE. HE SPARED HER LIFE, GAVE HER TO ME AS A SLAVE.

"ARDRA NURSED ME BACK TO HEALTH AND STAYED WITH ME FOR FOUR YEARS. BUT SHE WAS **NEVER** MY SLAVE.

"IN THE END, I FREED HER. SENT HER HOME TO GERMANIA. I NEVER THOUGHT TO SEE HER AGAIN."

AND NOW THE WOLF'S CUB HAS BECOME A SHE-WOLF.

YOU WERE ALWAYS TOO TENDERHEARTED, MARCUS. THE GREATEST GLADIATOR ROME HAS EVER KNOWN, MY PERSONAL BODYGUARD...

...BUT SOFT. DID OUR CAMPAIGNS IN NORTH AFRICA AND JUDEA TEACH YOU NOTHING.?

I LEARNED TO LOVE MY CAESAR, TRUST IN HIS WISDOM, SHARE HIS DRINK, KEEP MY SWORD WITHIN ARM'S REACH, AND CHIDE HIM WHEN HE IS WRONG. IS THAT NOT ENOUGH.?

HAHAHAHA. WELL SAID. AND WHAT NOW SHALL CAESAR DO WITH THE WOLF BITCH?

÷SNIFF SNIFF÷

CAESAR!

HAHAHA HAHAHA!!! HE WHO LAUGHS LAST, CAESAR!

YOU AND ARDRA CAN TRAVEL THE ROAD TO HADES TOGETHER!

I WILL CRUSH THE ROMAN COHORT THAT AWAITS YOU BEYOND THE RHINE AND TAKE THE SILVER.

THEN I WILL TURN ALL GERMANIA INTO A ROMAN GRAVEYARD!

CAESAR. THE REST OF YOU! GET BACK!

THAT ONE FIGHTS LIKE A **FURY!**

IF HE FALLS, THE REST WILL BE EASY!

MARCUS! YOUR **BACK!**

URRRRK!

HUMPH. A TRAITOR.

NOT A SWORDS-MAN.

ENOUGH! THIS BATTLE IS OVER. I, CAESAR, COMMAND IT! THROW DOWN YOUR WEAPONS.

YOUR WORDS HAVE **POWER,** CAESAR.

A SINGLE CAESAR IS WORTH **TEN THOUSAND** WARRIORS.

AND WILL YOUR TEN THOUSAND STAND AGAINST THE BITCH AND HER WOLF PACK HERE AND NOW?

YOU WOULD FETCH A GREAT RANSOM.

ARDRA!

PEACE, MARCUS. SHE IS RIGHT. I WOULD FETCH THE GREATEST RANSOM, ARDRA ONE-HAND.

BUT YOU WILL FIND THAT I AM WORTH MORE TO YOU FREE AND IN ROME THAN CAPTIVE HERE IN GERMANIA.

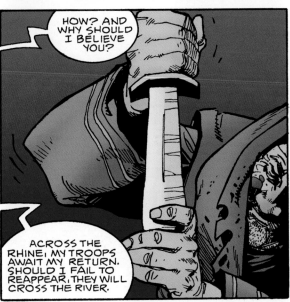

HOW? AND WHY SHOULD I BELIEVE YOU?

ACROSS THE RHINE, MY TROOPS AWAIT MY RETURN. SHOULD I FAIL TO REAPPEAR, THEY WILL CROSS THE RIVER.

THEY MAY NOT FIND YOU, BUT THEY WILL SLAUGHTER EVERY LIVING THING FOR LEAGUES AROUND.

AND THIS IS YOUR OFFER? YOU THINK BATAVIANS ARE AFRAID OF DYING?

VESPASIAN!

HE'S GONE.

NEVER HAVE I KNOWN HIS LIKE.

NOR EVER SHALL AGAIN. ROME'S GREATEST WARRIOR. AND RIGHT AS ALWAYS. IT *IS* TIME FOR WISDOM.

THE WISDOM OF *THREATS*, CAESAR?

IF I AM WISE ENOUGH TO EXTEND IT, I THINK YOU ARE WISE ENOUGH TO TAKE THE PROFFERED HAND OF FRIENDSHIP INSTEAD OF THE BLOODY SWORD OF WAR.

I WILL WITHDRAW MY LEGIONS BEYOND THE RIVER RHINE.

GUARD THE BORDER AS MY ALLY.

YOU WOULD HAVE *US* SECURE ROME'S BORDER?

IN YOUR OWN WAY, OF COURSE. A BUFFER AGAINST THOSE TRIBES WHO WOULD ATTACK ROME THROUGH GERMANIA.

YOU THINK I WILL DO THIS FOR MARCUS'S SAKE?

I HOPE MARCUS'S WORDS MAY PERSUADE YOU THAT I CAN BE TRUSTED, ARDRA ONE-HAND. THE THREE TALENTS OF SILVER MY CO-HORT GUARDS ACROSS THE RIVER WILL PERSUADE YOU THAT I AM SERIOUS.

I THOUGHT TO DO BUSINESS HERE WHEN I LEFT ROME. I SIMPLY WASN'T SURE WITH WHOM.

HAIL, CAESAR.

ARDRA, **LOOK!**

THE TRAITOR'S PORTION.

THROW HIS BODY TO THE WOLVES. THE COIN WITH IT.

AND AS THE MOON RISES BEYOND THE FOREST...

"CAESAR? WHO IS LUCIA? I NEVER HEARD MARCUS SPEAK THAT NAME BEFORE."

"HIS WOMAN. SHE WAS VERY BEAUTIFUL. THE MOST BEAUTIFUL WOMAN IN ALL THE EMPIRE, IT WAS SAID.

"SHE DIED OF PLAGUE THE YEAR OF SUETONIUS PAULINUS'S TRIUMPH.

"THAT IS WHY MARCUS ENTERED THE GAMES.

"HE HAD NOT FOUGHT PROFESSIONALLY FOR YEARS. HE EXPECTED TO BE KILLED.

"YOUR BRAVERY, YOUR FIERCE COURAGE SAVED HIM. IT WAS HIS GREATEST VICTORY."

"ONLY TO SEE HIM DIE HERE."

"THE FATES SUMMON US ALL EVENTUALLY, ARDRA.

"HE WOULD NOT REGRET THIS DEATH, AS YOU AND I DO. FAR BETTER THAN DYING AS LION FODDER IN THE COLOSSEUM.

"FOR HIS SAKE, YOU AND I...WE WILL MAKE SOMETHING OF THIS DAY. A PAX ROMANA IN THE WILDERNESS.

"MAY HE, TOO, FIND PEACE BEYOND OCEANUS IN THE FIELDS OF ELYSIUM. MAY LUCIA BE WAITING FOR HIM."

HAIL, MARCUS.

THE FIRE BURNED THROUGH THE NIGHT.

THE GRAY DAWN BROUGHT A HINT OF SNOW.

THEY STAYED TILL ONLY ASH REMAINED.

FIN

1000 AD
THE VIKING PRINCE

In 793 AD, the Vikings came out of the north to raid the coastlines of Europe with an unparalleled ferocity. Aboard their dragon ships, they sailed into the Mediterranean and across the ocean to the New World, plundering, trading and colonizing as they went. Their gods were as wild as the northlands from which they hailed. The Viking warriors feared no foe and looked to die in battle, to be carried by Odin's Valkyries into Valhalla. Always, they strove against fate.

In that struggle, some became legends.

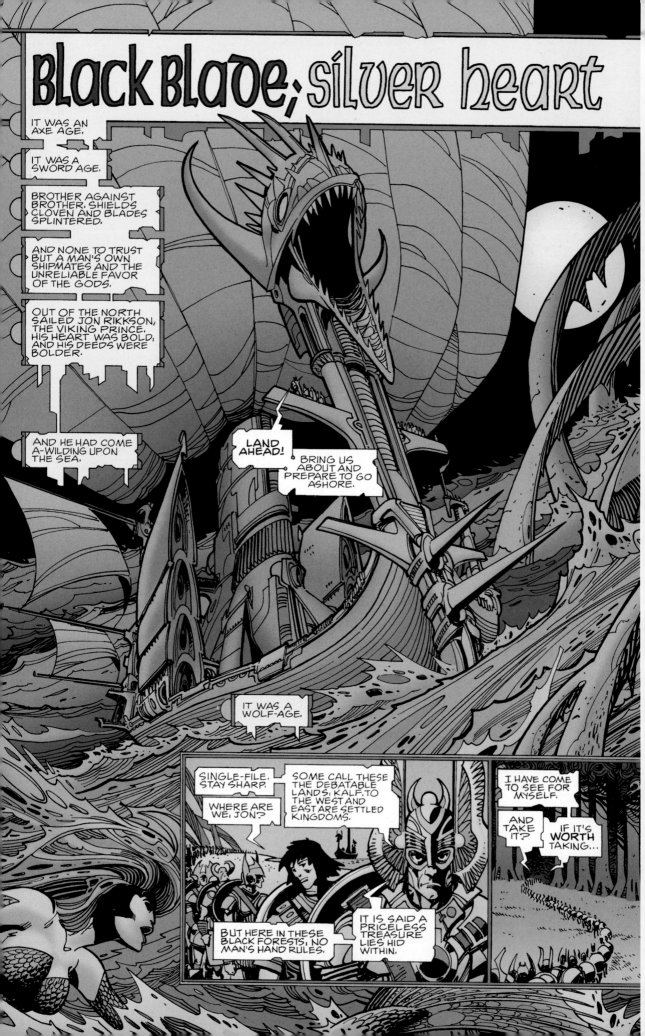

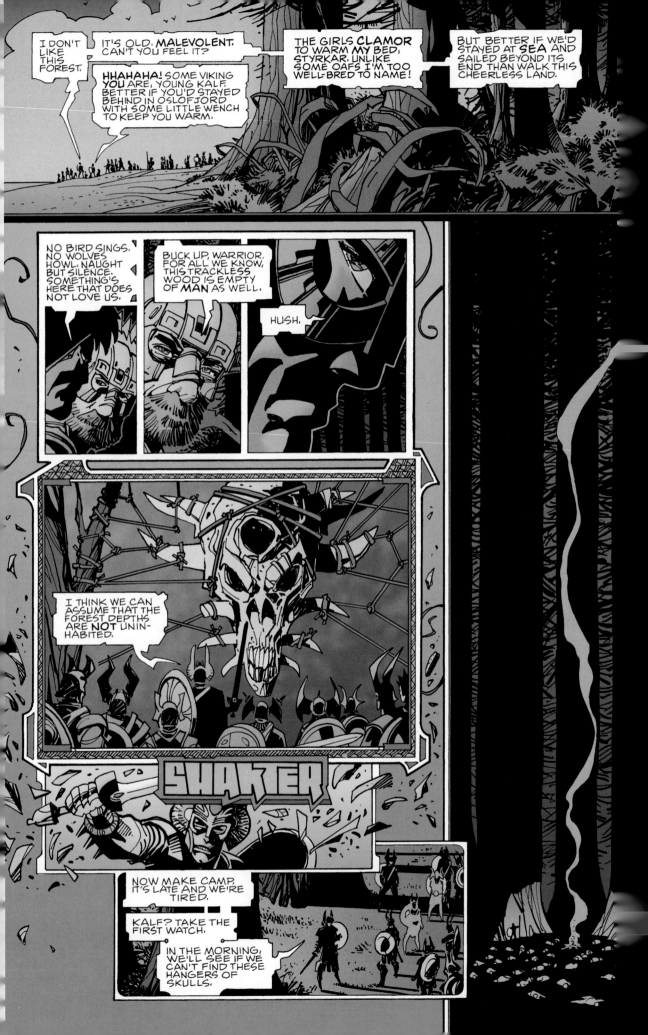

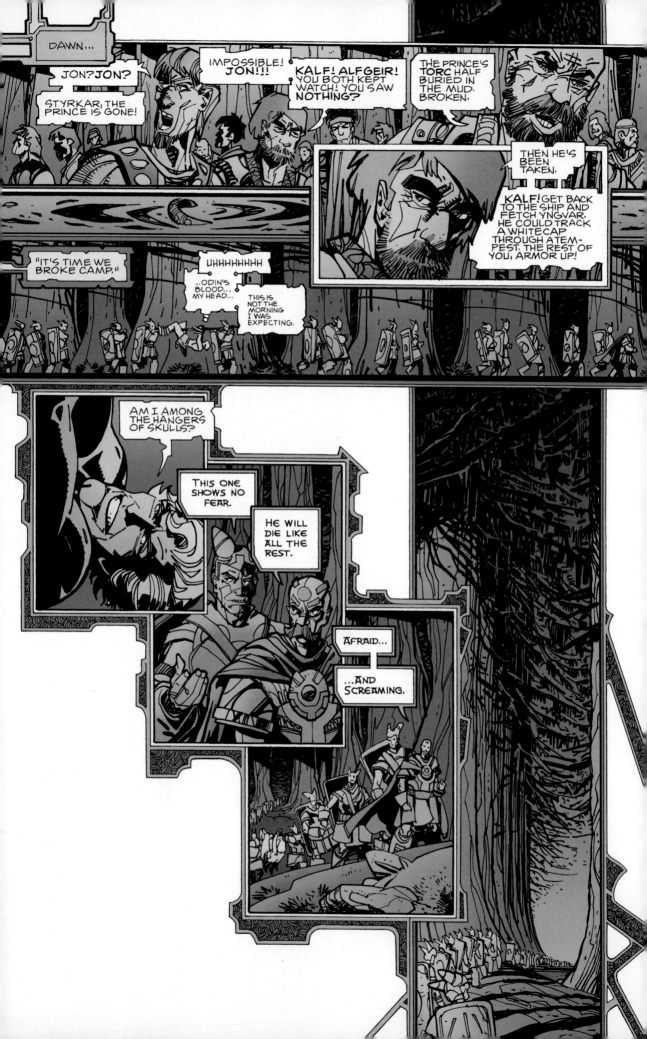

THE SUSURRATION
OF THE WIND
THROUGH THE TREE-
TOPS IS THE ONLY
SOUND.

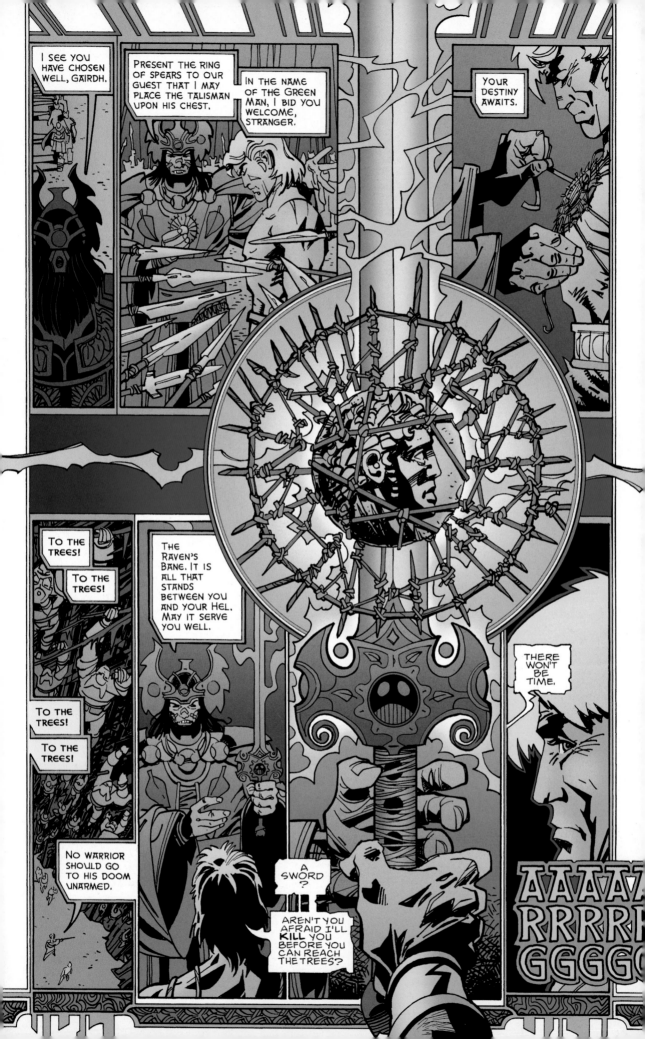

1720 AD
CAPTAIN FEAR

From the 16th to the 18th centuries, the coast of the Caribbean was known as the Spanish Main. The waters of the New World were a Spanish sea, across which sailed the great treasure fleets, taking the wealth of Empire home to Madrid. But the fleets did not sail unmolested. Piracy flourished; men's lives depended on the cannonball, the cutlass, and the wind. Buccaneers were the scourge of the Spanish Main. And the most daring and ruthless of them all was Captain Fear.

KKRACK!

ANY MAN DON'T... *DIES!*

FEAR'S BEEN IN THE DINGHY FOR FIVE DAYS. HE AIN'T DEAD TOMORROW MORNING, WE'LL HAUL IN THE DINGHY AND PUT AN END TO HIM THERE AND THEN.

I'LL SPLIT HIS RIBS AND PULL HIS BEATIN' HEART RIGHT OUT HIS BODY!

THEN IT'S THE SPANISH MAIN AND TREASURE SHIPS FER US, ME LADS!

NOW, YE GENTLE-MEN OF FORTUNE! ARE YE WITH ME?

AYE, CAP'N!

AYE! AYE!

AYE!

WE'LL TURN THIS OCEAN RED WITH SPANISH BLOOD!

shrigg

shriggg

shrigggg

shrig

thpiikt!

HE'S DONE.

AND SO ARE YOU, IF YOU DO SOMETHING *STUPID* LIKE THAT AGAIN, BULL!

NO POINT IN NOT *PROFITING* FROM THIS BIT OF BAD BUSINESS.

GRAB THE LAST OF THE GEAR AND RUN. THE TIDE IS WITH US, AND WE'D BEST BE ON IT!

CAST OFF, CERVANTES, AND *CROWD* ON THE SAIL!

BULL'S KILLED SOMEONE AND OUR FREEDOM IS ABOUT TO BE MEASURED BY THE LENGTH OF A *CANNON* SHOT!

BOOOUM

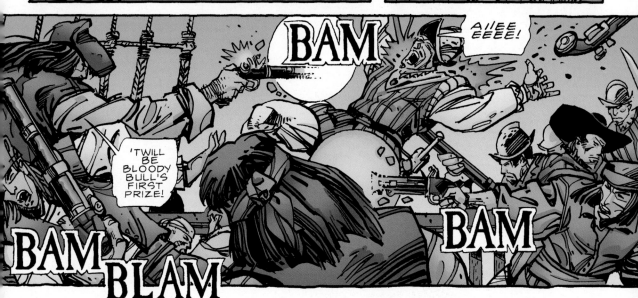

HOW IS THIS *POSSIBLE?* THEY WERE ALL *DEAD* MEN!

CAPTAIN, THE MAN O'WAR IS GOING TO OPEN FIRE ON US! WHAT SHOULD WE *DO,* SIR?

IF THEY CAPTURE US, THEY'LL HANG US FOR *SURE!*

RIGHT YOU ARE, MISTER STANDISH.

THKKAT

IF THEY CAPTURE US,

CAPTAIN?

SIR?

BOOM BOOOM BOOOUM BOOMBOOM BOOOM

THE EDGE IS DONE FOR, SIR. THEY'RE NOT EVEN FIRING BACK!

BREAKS MY HEART TO SEE HER GO LIKE THAT.

MINE, TOO, CERVANTES. BUT WE'LL SAIL THE SPANISH MAIN AGAIN, OLD FRIEND.

THE GALLEON'S TOO SLOW FOR PIRATES LIKE US. WE'LL MAKE FOR PORT ROYAL, AND WE'LL FIND ANOTHER SHIP THAT'S--

CAPTAIN, SIR! HAVE YOU *SEEN* WHAT SHE'S *CARRYIN'* IN HER *HOLD,* SIR?

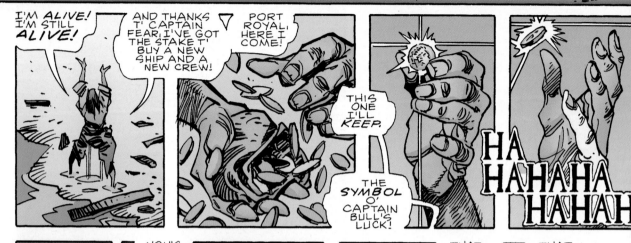

EPILOGUE

I'M ALIVE! I'M STILL ALIVE!

AND THANKS T' CAPTAIN FEAR, I'VE GOT TH' STAKE T' BUY A NEW SHIP AND A NEW CREW!

PORT ROYAL, HERE I COME!

THIS ONE I'LL KEEP.

THE SYMBOL O' CAPTAIN BULL'S LUCK!

HA HAHAHA HAHAH

BLAM

YOU'S RIGHT, JEAN. THAT WAS TH' GLINT O' GOLD!

MORE DOUBLOONS 'N I'VE EVER SEEN!

WE'LL SPLIT 'EM RIGHT DOWN THE MIDDLE, QUILL!

THAT SILVER COIN'S MIGHTY PRETTY.

I KILLED 'IM SO I'LL KEEP IT ME-SELF.

THAT SHOT MEANS YER PISTOL'S EMPTY, QUILL...

...AND I SAW THE SWABBIE FIRST.

SO HAND IT OVER.

YOU TOUCH THE HANDLE O' YER PISTOL, JEAN, I'LL CUT YER THROAT!

SKLICCKT
BLAMM!

FIN

1881 AD
BAT LASH

In 1877, prospector Ed Schieffelin discovered a rich vein of silver in the desolate hills east of the San Pedro River in the Arizona Territory. Within four years, Tombstone was a thriving boomtown of miners, barkeeps, gunfighters, prostitutes, assayers, cardsharps, and dry goods salesmen.

At night, honky-tonk pianos cranked out tuneless music to keep the saloon customers happy and drinking rotgut. Poker was the game of choice. It separated miners from their money, and sometimes men from their lives, as thousands of dollars changed hands at the turn of a card.

THAT *AIN'T* THE HAND YOU HAD-- I MEAN...

FFFFFF FFFFF!

I'LL *KILL* YOU, YOU *FOUR-FLUSHIN', DOUBLE-DEALIN'*--

ONLY REASON YOU'RE STILL *ALIVE,* IKE, IS 'CAUSE YOU'RE AS SLOW DRAWIN' AS YOU ARE SLOW-WITTED.

NOW DROP YOUR GUN AND BACK OUT O' HERE, CAREFUL-LIKE.

ANYBODY ELSE AT THE TABLE WISH TO DISCUSS MY GAMBLIN' ETHICS?

NO? WELL, I CAN TELL YOU TRUTHFULLY THAT THEY ARE NO WORSE'N *YOURS.*

YOU BOYS NEED TO IMPROVE SOME BEFORE YOU RISK YOUR HANDS AT A GAME O' CHANCE AGIN.

AND NOW, GENTLEMEN, I THINK THE TIME HAS COME FOR ME TO MAKE MY FAREWELLS AND DEPART YOUR LOVELY TOWN.

BUT I'D HATE TO BE A SORE WINNER. HOW ABOUT IF I LEAVE ENOUGH BEHIND TO COVER A COUPLE ROUNDS OF DRINKS?

NIKKY? BEST OF THE HOUSE FOR EVERYBODY. ON ME.

WHICH I EARNED JUST AS *FAIR* AND *SQUARE* AS THE GAME.

BUT... BUT YER TAKIN' *ALL OUR MONEY!*

YESSIR, MISTER LASH.

Y'SEE? IF YOU *DON'T* SHOOT ME, I'M DEAD. AND IF YOU *DO* SHOOT ME, I'M *STILL* DEAD, BUT THERE'LL BE A CROWD HERE IN NO TIME.

THEN YOU'RE GOING TO HAVE TO *SPLIT* THAT MONEY, FOUR WAYS, MAYBE *MORE.*

WHEREAS, IF YOU JUST TAKE IT, YOU WON'T HAVE TO SPLIT IT AT ALL.

AND IN RETURN FOR MY LIFE, I'LL LEAVE TOWN QUIETLY.

IT'S A DEAL!

NOW GET OUT O' HERE BEFORE I CHANGE MY MIND. IF'N I SEE YOU AGIN, I'LL KILL YA *ANYWAYS!*

WELL, EASY COME, EASY GO.

AS IKE'LL SHORTLY BE LEARNIN'.

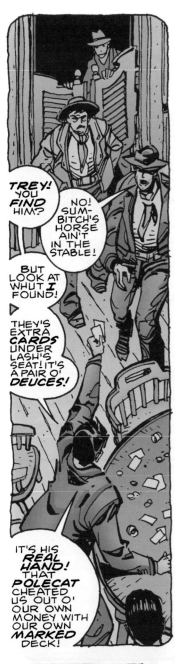

FIN

THE PRESENT
TWO-FACE

Gotham City—a teeming labyrinth of humanity filled with sunshine and shadow, where darkness feeds and flourishes in her secret ways... and where evil is held at bay only by the efforts of those who cross over into the shadow and stalk the night.

Sometimes, it isn't enough.

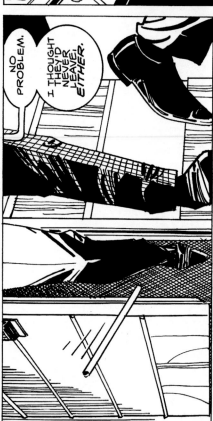

To enormous ... Museum of would be Coin Gotham Historical that ... The Sehler held night with an exhibition ... privately ancient of King Midas! ... the largest privately ancient envy ... the largest from the first time in Collection, of coinage for the glitterati assemblage went on display as the private Lear world, ... was tight and private Lear 97 years. Security was tight with some of ... arrived in their limousines seen with some of ... and be ... Bruce Wayne, ... for many

pieces of ... coin with ... shopping man ... A coin shekel was the ... curator. the ... 1970s. provenance, for a new shopping mall ... Arizona, in ... about its ... excavations ...

Rare Coin Exhibit at Gotham Museum

Shipment of Arms Hijacked!

Associated Gotham Wire

Eagle Overland Shipping reported today that one of their 18-wheelers carrying a cargo of pistols, intended for the U.S. Army, was hijacked yesterday evening near Moriarty, New Mexico. The hijacking occurred when two armed masked men accosted the driver as he was climbing into his rig after a break at a truck stop north of town. The driver was forced to park the truck well off Interstate 40 at an abandoned gas station, tying up the driver with duc... offloaded the weapons in...

...firearms in the day in Edgewood that both vans were military versions of... unconfirmed reports with laser sights program, as...

Beretta 92, a 9mm semi-automatic...

Museum Attendance Spikes Big Time

...ss experienced ...usual surge in attendance in the last few weeks. Museum Director Julianna Arms attributed the increase to a unexpected degree of public interest in the Sehler Coin Collection exhibit that opened last week. "I'm a little taken aback by the reaction," said Dr. Arms, "but very gratified. A generous grant from the Wayne Foundation enabled us to di...

...several attendees who have tried ... touch the exhibits. "No harm, no foul," smiled guard Bruce Pettijohn. "...l overexcited."

...enthusiasm has been so pronounced that the Museum has had to increase the number of guards posted during museum hours. Th...

The Coin Flip and Mental Balance In Decision-Making

The New Psychology
Dr Frances Rice

The Art of Effective Decision-Making has long been the focus of speculation, intense study, and applied statistical mathematics. We make decisions constantly, about sports, mate selection, verdict resolution, what flavor of ice cream to bring home. Yet the process of effective decision? Is it possible that a simple flip of a coin could enable us to reach decisions more quickly and more wisely? It is a matter not only of probabilities but of new access to our interior selves, an access that will allow us to understand how we truly feel about what we are about to make

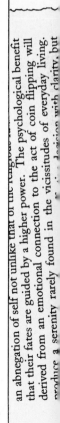

an abnegation of self not unlike that of the religious... The psychological benefit that their fates are guided by a higher power. The psychological benefit derived from an emotional connection to the act of coin flipping will produce a serenity rarely found in the vicissitudes of everyday living. ...decision with clarity, but

Breaking Bad Habits
A Guide
Mme. Mareskiya Foundation for Higher Knowledge
by Laura P.: first adept

...fall victim to bad habits, ranging of personal responsibility. But we need not suffer such habits in silence. It is within our power to change our habits and ourselves.

Begin by examining your daily life carefully. Are there things you do that annoy others? Things that others do that annoy you? Things that prevent you from reaching your full potential? That stand between you and peace of mind? A careful examination of your daily routine will undoubtedly reveal a dozen minor irritations that you may not have noticed before, but that keep you...

...is not easy... group, friends who understand and will not judge you, but will offer them help during particularly difficult times of stress. With these tools in hand, anyone can remake himself or herself into the person they would like to be, to become all that...

last night. A heavily armed band of men broke into the Museum through a skylight at about 2:20 a.m. Apparently, they were attempting to steal the Sehler Coin Collection, an extremely valuable exhibit of ancient coinage, currently on display in the new Midas wing of the Museum.

Police were alerted by reports of gunfire heard from within the Museum at about 2:30 a.m. and arrived in force some ten minutes later. There are reports that they found several dead bodies, purportedly those of the robbers themselves.

There are also unconfirmed reports that the Batman was present at some point during the violence.

the exhibit's curator, Dr. Jorge Hupac, took inventory of the collection amidst the damage. Despite the fact that there are numerous coins worth hundreds of thousands of dollars, only a single coin was found to be 'iba shekel, was minted in the eastern

2087 AD
MANHUNTER 2070

It is the future.

The citizens of a brave new world zip to work in their flying cars, leave domestic chores to robots, and travel to the stars. But even in the future, the stars are a long way from Earth, and the frontiers are dangerous and largely unguarded. Those who journey outward risk everything.

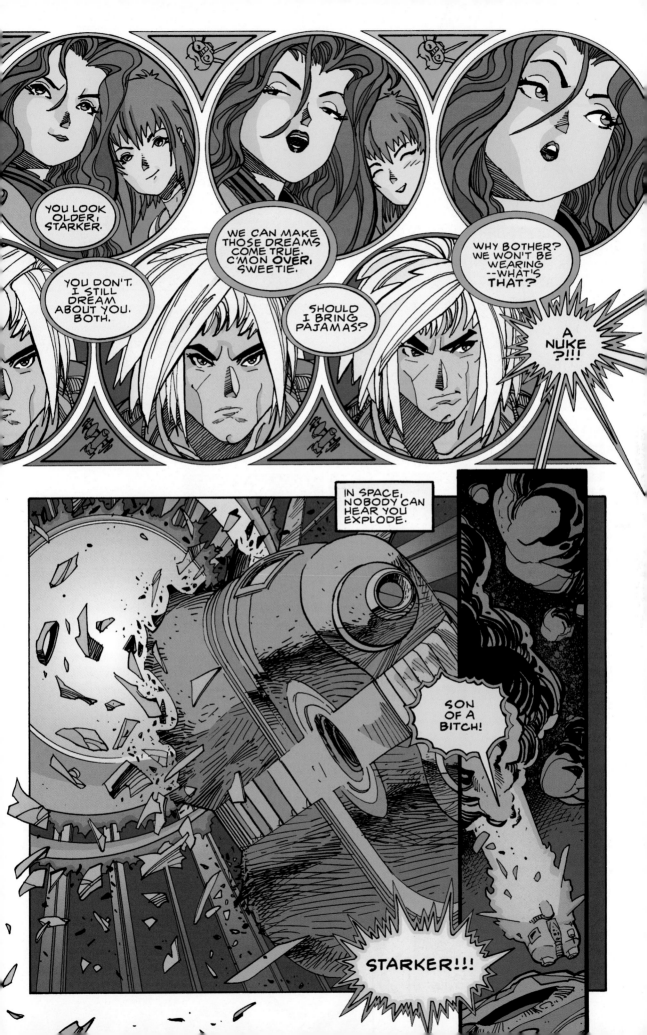

THE CHUGBOAT'S OLD, BUT SHE'S WELL BUILT.

SHE GOES IN WITH HER OUTER SHELL BREACHED...

...BUT HER INNER HULL HOLDING AT 77% INTEGRITY.

THEY **MIGHT** STILL BE ALIVE.

STARKER...

YES, GLORI?

DON'T DO ANYTHING STUPID.

ROGER THAT, FOLD ME ONTO THE BRIDGE.

FOLDD

BRRAKK!

NOTHING ELSE MOVES...

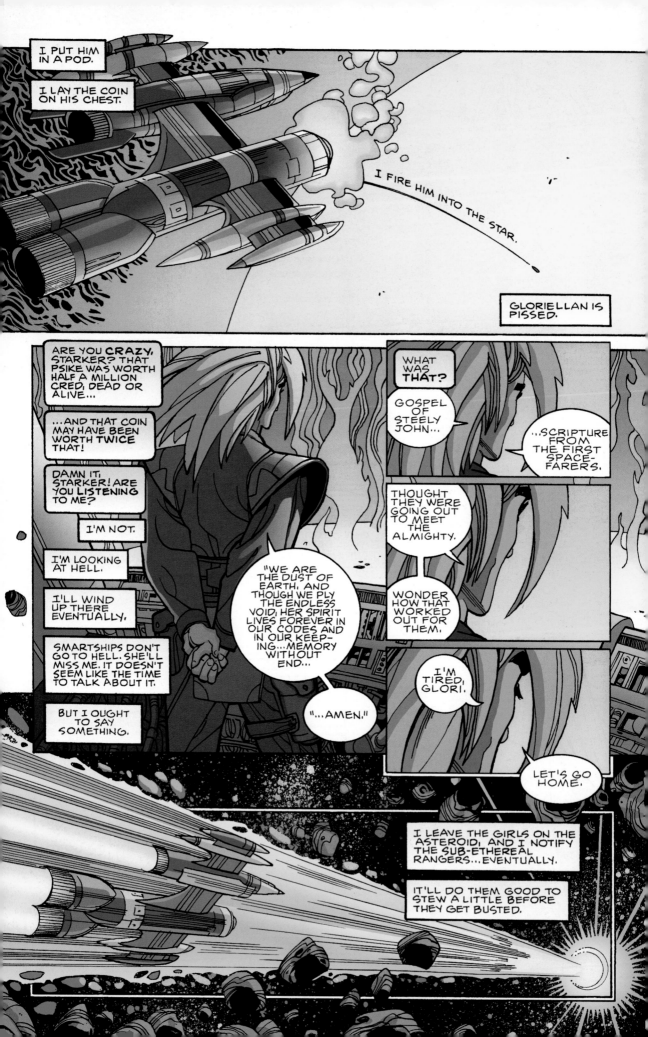

DESIGNATED K-TYPE STARS ON THE MAIN SEQUENCE ARE STABLE FOR **BILLIONS** OF YEARS.

THIRTEEN DAYS AFTER I'D FOLDED AND GONE HOME, JUST AS A RANGER PHANTOM MKIII WAS SETTING DOWN ON THE ASTEROID, RALPHA-B BLEW NOVA.

THE WHOLE SYSTEM VANISHED IN A HEARTBEAT OF RAGING FURY.

THERE WAS NOTHING LEFT.

I DON'T SEE LEDORA AND FENETTE IN MY DREAMS ANYMORE...

...BUT SOMETIMES, WHEN IT'S LATE AND I'M LYING IN MY BED ALONE...

...I STILL SMELL THEIR PERFUME.

The End

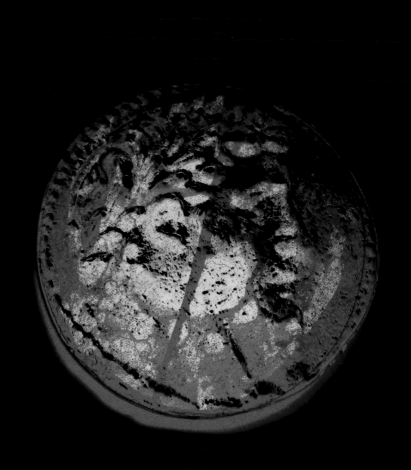

THE JUDAS COIN

SKETCH GALLERY

Bat Lash — the first drawing I did for The Judas Coin. Bat Lash was the first character I thought of in connection with the book, and the first plot I wrote. This was a presentation piece to go along with the proposal. I liked the logo so I lettered it into the opening sequence of the book.

Left: The original cover sketch for the book, the last drawing I did for the project. I wanted to place an image from each of the stories somewhere in the drawing. I altered the arrangement of the Two-Face head and the Batman figure slightly in the finished piece.

Below left: The structure drawing for the Batman for the cover, where I worked out the pose, mass, and lighting for the figure.

Below right: The structure drawing for the Two-Face head on the cover. The entire head isn't visible in the finished piece, but it's useful to work out the complete structure of an object before cropping it. Helps keep the drawing balanced. Below it is a pirate ship running before the wind, a small element in the cover drawing.

The Captain's cabin of the Reaper's Edge as the mutineers burst in. This page is essentially a study in storytelling, composition, 18th century costumes and weaponry, the interiors of an old sailing ship, and texture.

ILL-GOTTEN GAINS

A HOT SUMMER NIGHT IN TOMBSTONE, THE TERRITORY OF ARIZONA...

...THE IRONHORSE SALOON.

THE ONLY SOUNDS ARE THE LABORED BREATHING OF THE MEN AT THE TABLE...

...AND THE OCCASIONAL CLINK OF A SHOT GLASS FULL OF ROTGUT AT THE BAR.

EVEN THE UP-STAIRS ROOMS ARE EMPTY.

AND THEN THE SILENCE IS BROKEN.

I'LL RAISE YOU ANOTHER FIVE HUNDRED, IKE. YOUR MOVE.

A saloon in the old West. The imagery in the drawing owes a lot to every Western comic book I ever read.